The Promise of
Cognitive Psychology

The Promise of
Cognitive Psychology

Richard E. Mayer
UNIVERSITY OF CALIFORNIA, SANTA BARBARA

W. H. FREEMAN AND COMPANY
San Francisco

Project Editor: Judith Wilson

Copy Editor: Sean Cotter

Designer: Sharon H. Smith

Production Coordinator: William Murdock

Illustration Coordinator: Cheryl Nufer

Artist: Ron Newcomer

Compositor: Composition, etc.

Printer and Binder: The Maple-Vail Book Manufacturing Group

Library of Congress Cataloging in Publication Data

Mayer, Richard E   1947-
   The promise of cognitive psychology.

   (Series of books in psychology)
   Includes bibliographical references and index.
   1. Cognition.   I. Title.
   BF311.M427   153.4   80-39997
   ISBN 0-7167-1275-X
   ISBN 0-7167-1276-8 (pbk.)

Printed in the United States of America

1 2 3 4 5 6 7 8 9

Dedicated to Beverly, Kenny, and Davey

Contents

Preface

This book is intended to serve as a brief introduction to the major themes in cognitive psychology. It describes each of the major analytic tools that have been developed during the last few decades and shows how they can be applied to practical problems that are familiar to the reader. Instead of trying to survey and condense the research currently going on in cognitive psychology, I have provided representative examples of experimental and theoretical work in several key areas.

Readers need not have any previous background in experimental psychology. This book is intended as an adjunct text for courses in introductory psychology; for example, it can be used as a counterbalance for short books on behaviorism such as Skinner's *About Behaviorism* (1974), often used in such courses. It can also be used as an adjunct text for courses in topics such as human learning and memory, cognitive psychology, educational psychology, or problem solving. The general reader who is interested in learning more about the cognitive revolution in psychology will also find it useful.

There is encouraging evidence that the cognitive revolution, born in the late 1950s and early 1960s, has matured greatly during the 1970s. Early works such as *A Study of Thinking* (Bruner, Goodnow, and Austin, 1956), *Plans and the Structure of Behavior* (Miller, Galanter, and Pribram, 1960), and *Cognitive Psychology* (Neisser, 1967) set a tone and a direction that have recently produced some exciting advances. During the past decade there has been a virtual explosion both in the amount of new information and in the sophistication of our explanations of the mechanisms of human learning, memory, and cognition. One of the most significant departures from earlier work in cognitive psychology is that psychologists have become interested in explaining human learning, memory, and cognition within real-world domains. This book, therefore, briefly describes the newly developed cognitive analysis techniques and shows how they can be applied to several real-world problems.

The book is organized into five chapters. The first chapter provides a general overview and history of the cognitive approach to psychology. Each of the subsequent four chapters describes one of the major analytic tools of cognitive psychology, and is organized in the following way:

Problem. First, some familiar problem is presented, such as the question of what is involved in verbal ability tests (Chapter 2), solving arithmetic problems (Chapter 3), reading a story (Chapter 4), or solving algebra equations (Chapter 5).

Traditional Approach. Second, the traditional psychological approach to the problem is presented for the purpose of comparison with the cognitive approach.

Cognitive Approach. Third, the appropriate cognitive tool is described in some detail, including the information processing model (Chapter 2), the process model (Chapter 3), the structure model (Chapter 4), and the means–ends strategy analysis (Chapter 5).

Examples of the Cognitive Approach. The fourth section of each chapter demonstrates how the cognitive tool can be applied to a particular problem. Special care was taken to use examples that are familiar and at the same time demonstrate the advances that can be made using the cognitive approach. These include applying the information processing model to the study of ability (Chapter 2), using process models to describe arithmetic performance (Chapter 3), using structure models to describe reading comprehension performance (Chapter 4), and using means–ends analysis models to describe algebraic problem solving (Chapter 5).

Applying What You've Learned. The fifth section in each chapter gives you a chance to try your model-building expertise so that you can make sure you understand the main ideas presented.

Further Applications. Finally, each chapter closes with some comments concerning future trends and possible extensions of ideas presented in the chapter.

• • •

This book took shape during my sabbatical leave at the Learning Research and Development Center (LRDC), University of Pittsburgh. I am grateful for the hospitality and stimulating atmosphere provided at LRDC by Jim Greeno, Bob Glaser, Lauren Resnick, Jim Voss, Michi Chi, Paul Feltovich, Joan Heller, Mary Riley, Sherm Tyler, and many others. I also appreciated the many useful conversations with Jill Larkin and her colleagues at Carnegie-Mellon University. While these people cannot be held responsible for any shortcomings in this book, it does seem appropriate that this book evolved in Pittsburgh, which has produced much of the pioneering work in cognitive psychology. Finally, I would like to thank my parents, James and Bernis Mayer, and my brothers, Robert and Bernie Mayer, for their much appreciated encouragement; and Beverly, Kenny, and Davey for putting up with me while I worked on this project.

October 1980   Richard E. Mayer

Note to the Reader

In my role as psychology teacher, or as conversationalist at a cocktail party, or even at family gatherings, I am often in the position of having to answer the question, "Exactly what is cognitive psychology?" I find that many people believe psychology consists mainly of putting little white laboratory rats into mazes and putting neurotic people on the therapist's couch. For example, at the beginning of each term I like to ask my introductory psychology class to indicate who they already know in psychology. Almost everyone recognizes the names "Freud" and "Skinner"; however, these are usually the only universally recognized names in psychology.

The purpose of this little book, then, is to introduce a third approach to psychology—cognitive psychology. Even if you already know something about the behaviorist and Freudian theories, you will probably be interested in learning about the cognitive approach as well. Cognitive psychology deserves your attention for several reasons, which I will outline briefly.

Widespread. First, the cognitive approach has become so widespread that it is now a dominant theme in modern psychology. It has had an impact on a wide range of topics in psychology, including how we store and process information, how we form friendships and prejudices, how we think and reason, and how we respond to reinforcement. You cannot have a complete and accurate view of modern psychology without some basic knowledge of cognitive psychology.

Current. Second, cognitive psychology is relatively new, having taken hold only within the last 10 or 20 years. Since it is much newer than either the behaviorist or psychoanalytic approaches, the cognitive approach represents a fresh viewpoint in modern psychology.

Promising. Third, because it offers a new perspective, a way of looking at human behavior from the inside, cognitive psychology offers some promise of furthering psychology both as a science and as a means of promoting human welfare. It has already changed the way we look at questions like: What is intelligence? How do we learn when we read? How do children learn arithmetic? Why are some people good problem solvers? This book focuses primarily on the promising tools and techniques in cognitive psychology that can be applied to these kinds of practical problems.

The Promise of
Cognitive Psychology

1 Introduction to Cognitive Psychology

DEFINITION OF COGNITIVE PSYCHOLOGY

What is cognitive psychology? If you asked several different psychologists this question, you probably would not always get the same answer. Some might try to describe how cognitive psychology is different from other approaches such as the behaviorist or psychoanalytic approaches. Some might emphasize the topics that cognitive psychologists generally study, such as human memory, perception, problem solving, learning, and so forth. Some might emphasize the general theoretical framework that underlies cognitive psychology. This framework—called the information processing model—views all humans as active processors of information; it will be discussed in detail in Chapter 2.

In spite of these conflicting answers to the simple question "What is cognitive psychology?" I think most psychologists would agree on the following very general definition: *Cognitive psychology is the scientific analysis of human mental processes and memory structures in order to understand human behavior.* Let's examine each component of this definition in turn.

Scientific analysis. The first part of the definition refers to the "how" of cognitive psychology. Only the methods of science may be used. This means, for example, that the data we use must be public—any reasonable person should be able to find the same data by following the same procedure. Thus, your own intuitions and feelings about how your mind works are not acceptable bases for cognitive psychology unless you can formulate a prediction that is directly observable by others. This makes the task of cognitive psychology quite indirect—we cannot observe private mental events but can only infer them from someone's behavior. Thus, cognitive psychologists must devise scientific methods to observe mental life indirectly. The principal tools of cognitive psychology involve precise analytic techniques for breaking mental activities down into measurable parts. These tools will be outlined at the end of this chapter.

Mental processes and structures. This part of the definition concerns the "what" of cognitive psychology. The object of study is human mental life. Cognitive psychology studies what is going on inside a person's head when he or she is performing some task —that is, mental processes—and the way a person stores knowledge and uses it in performing some task—that is, mental structures.

Understanding human behavior. The final part of the definition concerns the "why" of cognitive psychology. The goal of cognitive psychology is to produce a clear and accurate description of internal cognitive events and knowledge so that we can better predict and understand human behavior. For example, we study the processes underlying arithmetic problem solving so that eventually we can better predict and understand why some children succeed and some fail in learning simple arithmetic.

THREE PSYCHOLOGIES

It will help you put cognitive psychology into perspective if you assume that there are really many different approaches to psychology. Although this section will focus on three major approaches, you may acquaint yourself with other schools in psychology by referring to the Suggested Readings at the end of this chapter. This section will examine behaviorism (as represented by Skinner), psychoanalytic theory (as represented by Freud), and cognitivism (the subject of this book). In order to understand cognitive psychology you should have some idea how it differs from the alternative approaches.

In the previous section it was noted that cognitive psychology has the following characteristics: Its subject matter is human mental or rational activity; its methods involve the scientific analysis of mental structures and processes; and its goal is the understanding of human behavior.

Let's see how behaviorism stands on each of these three points. First, like cognitive psychology, behaviorism has as its goal the understanding of human behavior. However, unlike cognitive psychology, there is no attempt to understand the internal processes that underly behavior. Second, like cognitive psychology, behaviorism is committed to the rigorous methods of science. However, it must be noted that the particular techniques used in cognitive psychology differ from those used in behaviorist approaches. Third, the major difference between behaviorism and cognitivism concerns the question of what should be the subject matter of psychology. Behaviorists (Skinner, 1953) argue that since internal mental events cannot be directly observed they can never be the legitimate objects of scientific study. Thus the subject matter of psychology must be restricted to what can be directly observed—behavior. Theories about unseen and unseeable mechanisms supposedly underlying behavior have no place because these mental processes and structures cannot be directly observed. According to behaviorists, in order for psychology to be a rigorous, useful. science it must use scientific methods to develop laws of behavior.

The cognitive approach differs from behaviorism mainly on the issue of whether or not it is useful to study mental processes and structures that cannot be directly seen. The cognitive response to the behaviorist position is not that it is wrong, but rather that it is too limiting and restricting. In order to fully understand human behavior it is necessary to understand the mechanisms that underlie behavior. Cognitive theories must be subjected to rigorous testing and changed when the predictions of a theory don't match the actual behavior. However, cognitive theories do have a place in psychology as long as they are stated in a way that allows for some direct, observable test. For example, if the behaviorist approach were applied to other sciences, like chemistry and physics, there could be no theory of atomic structure. Some of the entities making up an atom cannot be seen, yet a theory of atoms can make useful predictions. The same can be said for a germ theory of disease, since germs had not yet been observed at the time of the invention of the germ theory.

Now, let's see how the psychoanalytic approach compares with the others. First, the goal is the same as in cognitive psychology and behaviorism: to understand human behavior. Second, like the behaviorists and cognitivists, the psychoanalytic approach often purports to use scientific methods. However, many criticisms have centered on the claim that the psychoanalytic approach has not yet developed methods of sufficient rigor and power, and that consequently it must often resort to nonscientific methods (like intuition, clinical judgment, or untestable dogma). Third, the major difference between the psychoanalytic approach and the other approaches concerns what should be the subject matter of psychology. Like the cognitive approach, this approach emphasizes the study of internal mechanisms that underlie behavior; however, while cognitive psychologists tend to study the rational or intellectual side of mental life, the psychoanalytic approach emphasizes internal feelings, emotions, and desires. These are very much more difficult to study than the rational side of human mental life, and the necessary analytic techniques have yet to be developed.

Box 1.1 summarizes the similarities and differences among the three psychologies described in this section. They all purport, with varying degrees of success, to use scientific methods and to have as a goal the understanding of human behavior. They differ with respect to the particular tools they use and the subject matter they use the tools on. The behaviorists focus on well-controlled studies of human behavior, the cognitivists study the processes and structures that make up the rational, intellectual side of mental life, and the psychoanalysts focus on the irrational, emotional side of mental life. Certainly, a complete psychology of humans requires that all three components—behavior, cognition, and affect—be clearly understood and related to one another. Hopefully, as psychology progresses, the best features of each approach will be blended into a unified science.

	Uses scientific methods	Goal is to understand human behavior	Research focus on
Behaviorism	Yes (well established)	Yes	Behavior
Cognitivism	Yes (newly established)	Yes	Cognition
Psychoanalytic approach	Sometimes (not yet well established)	Yes	Affect

Box 1.1   Comparison of Three Psychologies

HISTORY OF COGNITIVE PSYCHOLOGY

A complete history of cognitive psychology is beyond the scope of this book. The Suggested Readings at the end of this chapter will help provide you with more detail. However, a summary of the ideas that have led up to the cognitive revolution in psychology will help you understand some of the apparently peculiar arguments and theories you might read about in psychology texts, and will help you appreciate why psychologists are doing the work they are doing today.

Wilhelm Wundt is generally cited as the founder of scientific psychology, and he certainly had a strong influence on the field for a generation or more. When Wundt established a psychology lab at the University of Leipzig in 1879, he also established an approach to psychology called structuralism. It was called structuralism because its goal was to study and analyze all the various parts of human consciousness. Wundt argued strongly that the new science of psychology must use the methods of science. However, the technique that he and his students relied on turned out to be a rather poor one. They used the method of introspection—trained introspectionists would carefully describe what went on inside their heads as they performed some task.

The method of introspection was open to so much abuse that it provoked a very strong reaction, especially in America. By the early 1900s a new movement was taking hold as a reaction against Wundt's structuralism. This movement, called behaviorism under the leadership of John Watson in America, became the dominant force in psychology by 1920, and like structuralism it held on for 30 years. Behaviorists claimed that the methods and subject matter of psychology had to be changed if it was to become a strong and respected science. The method of introspection was out; more rigorous and carefully controlled laboratory studies were in. The subject matter of consciousness was out because it was too nebulous; only behavior was considered the appropriate subject matter of psychology, since only behavior was directly observable. In retrospect, it appears that the behaviorists were certainly correct in emphasizing rigorous methods but perhaps were overzealous in ruling out the study of mental events.

A second reaction against Wundt's structuralism developed mainly in Europe at about the same time that behaviorism came to dominate American psychology. This reaction was called gestalt psychology. Unlike behaviorism, gestalt psychology kept mental processes and structures as the subject matter of psychology; however, like behaviorism it attempted to use rigorous scientific methods more powerful than introspection. Unfortunately, the rigorous tools of scientific analysis were just not available to gestalt psychologists, and eventually their failure to develop precise theories and methods, coupled with the freezing effects of Nazism in Europe, put an end to gestalt psychology. Many psychologists see gestalt psychology as a forerunner of cognitive psychology. The gestalt psychologists asked many of the same questions that cognitive psychologists ask today; however, today we like to think that we have the tools to answer at least some of them successfully.

Finally, a third major approach to psychology began to develop in Europe, mainly as a branch of medical science. In the early 1900s the problem of mental illness was finally being subjected to scientific analysis, and Freud's work in the early 1900s came to dominate the field. Freud's view was truly revolutionary, for he argued that human behavior—and he was especially interested in abnormal behavior—was caused by something that had happened to the patient. This is called the medical model because a mental illness was thought to have a locatable cause, just as physical illness does. Freud's work led to the development of psychoanalytic theory, which attempts to describe the mechanisms underlying human feelings and emotion. While many alternative theories and therapeutic techniques have come and gone since Freud's time, psychology is still seeking to understand the affective side of human beings.

By 1950 or so, the time was right for a change. The hold of behaviorism on American psychology was finally weakening after a 30-year reign. Gestalt psychology and psychoanalytic theory had been torn apart by the upheaval in Europe. The new electronic age was coming, bringing with it a device that would profoundly influence psychology—the computer.

By the late 1950s psychology was being influenced by ideas from at least three sources. First, the impact of the computer was beginning to be felt. Computers could do many of the things that humans did—learn, store, manipulate, and remember information as well as use language, solve problems, and reason. Papers like "Elements of a Theory of Human Problem Solving" (Newell, Shaw, and Simon, 1958) paved the way for recasting old psychological problems in terms of modern computer analogies. Interest in internal processes and structures was again legitimate, since they could be specified precisely in terms of a computer program. Second, in the field of linguistics there was a growing shift away from behaviorist theories of language and toward an analysis of the structures underlying comprehension and production of utterances. This shift was spearheaded by *Syntactic Structures* (Chomsky, 1957), a book that provided for a cognitive analysis of language behavior. A third force involved the growing impact of the work of Piaget (1954). Piaget focused on the growth of internal structures and processes that underlie developmental changes in human behavior. Thus in the computer (or artificial intelligence) approach of Simon, the psycholinguistic approach of Chomsky, and the biological approach of Piaget there was converging interest and success in describing internal cognitive processes and structures.

Even in traditional areas of psychology, the late 1950s were sprinkled with new and powerful ideas. In 1956 Bruner, Goodnow, and Austin provided a cognitive interpretation of the strategies involved in concept learning in a volume entitled *A Study of Thinking.* In the same year, Miller published a landmark paper, "The Magic Number Seven, Plus or Minus Two," which encouraged the development of the information processing model presented in Chapter 2.

In 1960 a book appeared called *Plans and the Structure of Behavior,* by Miller, Galanter, and Pribram. It offered a cognitive alternative to stimulus–response (S–R) behaviorism, and the cognitive revolution was called into action. The main idea in the book was that there were two ways of looking at behavior: (1) The S–R behaviorist approach was to say the unit of behavior is the stimulus–response association. In other words, each situation is associated with a response (or many responses). (2) The alternative approach was to say that the unit of behavior is a plan— a system for generating behavior similar to the feedback loops used in computers. In other words, behavior is generated by a set of mental processes and tests on the environment rather than specifically tied to an environmental stimulus. The human thus is transformed from a passive responder to stimuli into an active processor of information.

By 1967 there was enough research literature for Neisser to produce a well-integrated textbook called *Cognitive Psychology.* Thus, the first successful textbook on cognitive psychology not only built on the theoretical framework of Miller, Galanter, and Pribram (1960) but also provided an integrated summary of actual research. The theoretical contribution of Neisser's book was to posit a general information processing model consisting of a series of distinct memory stores and processes (see Chapter 2 for a further discussion of this model). The research contribution of Neisser's book was to show that it was possible to study internal mental processes using the precise tools of cognitive psychology. While Neisser dealt mainly with research on perception—the main interest of the structuralists and gestaltists, by the way—he also provided a framework for cognitive research in all areas of psychology.

By 1970 there was enough research going on in cognitive psychology that a journal with this name could be established and supported. But work in this area was not confined to one small journal or one small research area. During the 1970s the cognitive revolution came to influence all branches of psychology. What is new and interesting in many areas of psychology today is the application of the new techniques of cognitive psychology to old problems.

For example, in human experimental psychology the cognitive approach has come to dominate the way we understand how humans perceive, learn, remember, and reason. In developmental psychology the cognitive development of humans has become a major theme. Following the pioneering work of Jean Piaget, developmental psychologists have increasingly studied the changes in cognitive processes and cognitive representation of knowledge that occur with growth. In social and personality research, the concept of attribution has been a strong influence on recent research. Attribution refers to the cognitive process of trying to justify one's social behavior or that of someone else. Even in the traditional stronghold of behaviorism—animal learning —new work is progressing in the study of cognitive and memory processes in laboratory animals.

The history of cognitive psychology is summarized in Box 1.2. We can now return to the beginning of this brief history. As you may recall Wundt, in founding psychology, sought for his new science a better understanding of internal cognitive processes such as consciousness and attempted to analyze mental life into its parts. In these respects, cognitive psychology has returned to the origins of psychology. The gestaltists attempted to develop further the study of mental processes and structures; they asked fascinating questions about the nature of mental life but were never able to give fully satisfactory answers. Cognitive psychology has returned to many of these questions, with the hope that now—armed with better tools and years of experience— psychology may at last be able to come to grips with the issues that brought it into being. We still do not know whether this latest attempt to study the mechanisms underlying human behavior will succeed. There are promising signs that it has achieved much progress, and examples are given in the following chapters. As

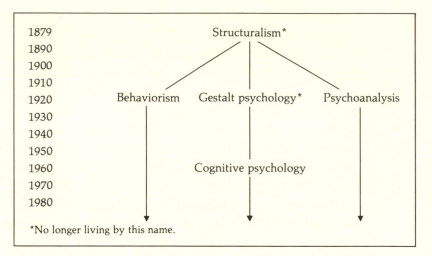

1879		Structuralism*	
1890			
1900			
1910			
1920	Behaviorism	Gestalt psychology*	Psychoanalysis
1930			
1940			
1950			
1960		Cognitive psychology	
1970			
1980			

*No longer living by this name.

Box 1.2   Summary of the History of Cognitive Psychology

you read these chapters you may think of psychology as returning to the questions posed by the structuralists and the gestaltists, but with one difference—we come equipped with analytic tools that have taken a century to develop. These tools will be described in the next section.

THE TOOLS OF COGNITIVE PSYCHOLOGY

As the previous section suggests, there is an interesting sense in which ideas circulate in psychology until we have the tools to deal with them. Certainly, modern cognitive psychology owes a debt to Wundt for his interest in human mental life. Yet he and his students, while they asked interesting questions, simply lacked the tools to test their ideas adequately. Similarly, cognitive psychology owes a debt to the gestaltists, who formulated many of the most interesting theories and questions in psychology concerning human mental life. Yet, like the structuralists, the gestaltists offered only vague theories and lacked the precise analytic tools to progress. Cognitive psychology even owes a debt to its two rivals—the behaviorist and psychoanalytic approaches—

because they provide constant reminders of what yet needs to be done. Certainly, cognitive psychology must eventually be able to go beyond theories of rational cognitive processes and incorporate the irrational, affective side of human life; and it cannot lose sight of the demand of the behaviorists for a true science based on scientific observation and testable theories.

What are the tools of cognitive psychology that allowed a successful rebirth of interest in cognitive processes? In this book, I will emphasize four major new tools. Each will be briefly described below.

Analysis of the information processing system. The first main tool is what can be called the "information processing model." This model is based on the idea that humans are processors of information: information comes in through our sense receptors, we apply a mental operation to it and thus change it, we apply another operation and change it again, and so on, until we have an output ready to be stored in memory or used to generate some behavior. The information processing model concerns the series of cognitive operations (or processes) that a person uses in a given situation, or to put it another way, the various organizations of information as it progresses through the system. As you may see, this model is based partly on a computer analogy. Humans are like computers in the sense that both can take information, operate on it, and generate some appropriate response. Thus, since computers can do many of the things that humans can do, we can describe the processes that go on inside the human mind in the same terms we use to describe the processes that go on inside the computer. There are certainly some problems with this analogy; for example, it ignores the fact that humans are alive, trying to survive, and full of emotions and feelings as well as intellect. However, put aside your reservations for a moment and first try to understand the information processing framework as described in Chapter 2. You will see what this tool is and how it can be applied to a recurrent issue in psychology—the nature of human intellectual abilities. After reading the next chapter you will be in a better position to judge for yourself whether the cognitive approach helps explain human mental life and behavior.

Analysis of cognitive processes. In addition to the general information processing model, there are more specific techniques for representing what is going on in a person's head while he or she is performing a given task. For example, what is the procedure children have in their heads when they finally learn long division? They have acquired some procedural knowledge that they did not have before. Cognitive psychology provides techniques for analyzing precisely what that new knowledge might be. In general, the analytic technique involves choosing an intellectual task like solving a long division problem, carefully observing and questioning how a person solves it, analyzing the process into small parts consisting of processes (things are manipulated) and decisions (a test is made), then testing the process model that is produced against the actual behavior of a human. The process model that is generated for a given task (like solving long division problems) may be written as a computer program or as a flow chart or in some other way. The techniques for producing a process model to represent someone's cognitive processes for a task and for testing the process model are laid out in Chapter 3. In particular, Chapter 3 shows how to analyze the cognitive processes involved in arithmetic and how to describe the knowledge that a person has in terms of a precise process model.

Analysis of cognitive structures. The previous paragraph introduced the idea of developing a process model to represent a person's procedural knowledge—knowledge about how to do something such as an arithmetic procedure. Another type of knowledge that can be represented using the analytic techniques of cognitive psychology is verbal knowledge—knowledge about some topic, such as a story. Techniques exist for representing the knowledge that a person has when he or she knows a story or some other piece of information. In general, these analytic techniques involve choosing some piece of information, presenting it to the subject as a passage to be read or listened to, then asking questions about the information such as asking the subject to recall it. The information is analyzed into its major parts and the relations between parts. This structure model can then be compared to the actual performance of the subject. The structure model that is created for a given passage may be represented as a tree diagram or as a network or in some other way. The techniques for specifying what people know when they know some verbal information are spelled out in Chapter 4. In particular, Chapter 4 shows how to analyze the cognitive structure acquired when a person learns a story and how to describe this knowledge as a precise structure model.

Analysis of strategies. So far we have mentioned techniques for analyzing the working of the general information processing system, for analyzing procedural knowledge into process models, and for analyzing verbal knowledge into structure models. The fourth major tool of cognitive psychology involves the investigation of techniques people use to control the various pieces of knowledge they have; such techniques are known as cognitive strategies. For example, consider the solution of an algebra problem, like "John drove 20 miles and used 2 gallons of gas. What was his gas mileage?" To answer this you need some verbal knowledge—namely, that mileage equals miles driven divided by the amount of gas used—some procedural knowledge—namely, how to divide—and an information processing system for holding the knowledge. However, in addition, you need a plan of attack, a strategy to help you achieve your goal. In general, cognitive psychologists have attempted to discover the strategies people use by giving them complex problems, asking them to describe their thinking process aloud, trying to develop a precise statement of the strategy (or heuristic) being used, and then testing the strategy model against actual human performance. One common strategy model is called means–ends analysis—a procedure that involves setting subgoals and then trying to find the means to achieve them. Means–ends analysis is more carefully described in Chapter 5, where it is applied to the task of solving algebra problems.

• • •

The remainder of this book describes each of the major tools of cognitive psychology in detail and provides examples of how these tools have been applied to real-world situations like reading and arithmetic. It is not intended to provide a broad survey of all the research results and theories in cognitive psychology, but rather to outline the major ideas in this new and exciting area. As you read the following chapters, your goal should simply be to get some idea of what the four cognitive tools are and to see whether or not you think they can be successfully applied to real situations.

SUGGESTED READINGS

Hilgard, E. R., and G. H. Bower. *Theories of learning.* Englewood Cliffs, N.J.: Prentice-Hall, 1980. An introduction to over a dozen major approaches to the study of human learning and behavior.

Humphrey, G. *Thinking: An introduction to its experimental psychology.* New York: Wiley, 1963. An excellent summary of the historical ideas and findings underlying modern cognitive psychology.

Mandler, J. M., and G. Mandler. *Thinking: From associationism to Gestalt.* New York: Wiley, 1964. A set of condensed readings from early studies in the psychology of cognition.

2 The Information Processing System

THE ABILITY PROBLEM

You have probably taken your share of standardized tests during the course of your school career. For example, you have probably taken one like the Scholastic Aptitude Test (SAT), which measures verbal and quantitative abilities and gives a score for each. To refresh your memory, read the passage given in Box 2.1 and then try to answer the questions. This type of test is typical of the items you would find on a standardized test of verbal ability.

Many of us are quick to accept these scores as evidence that we are "smart" or "dumb" in some ability. However, the question posed in this chapter is simply, what are the psychological mechanisms that allow one person to score high on tests of ability (such as that shown in Box 2.1) and another person to score low? These questions form the core of what can be called the *ability problem* —the problem of determining the differences in the cognitive system between people who differ in certain abilities.

People often make assessments of ability. For example, suppose someone told you that "Sue is a mathematical whiz" or "Tom knows everything about English." These sorts of assessments make sense because they tell us what performance to expect from Sue when she works on mathematical tasks or from Tom when he works on verbal tasks. You might translate these comments to mean that Sue has high mathematical ability or Tom has high verbal ability. However, the problem facing psychologists is to determine exactly what Tom has in his head that allows him to perform well on verbal tasks or what Sue has in her head that

Record your starting time: Hour _____ Minute _____ Second _____

The essential trick of the Renaissance pastoral poem, which was felt to imply a beautiful relation between rich and poor, was to make simple people express strong feelings in learned and fashionable language. From seeing elements of the two sorts of people combined like this the reader thought better of both; the best parts of each were used. The effect was in some degree to combine in the reader or the author the merits of the two sorts; he was made to mirror in himself more completely the effective elements of the society in which he lived. This was not a process that had to be explained in the course of writing pastoral poems; it was already shown in the clash between style and subject, and to make the clash work in the right way the writer had to keep up a firm pretense that he was unconscious of it.

The usual process for putting further meanings into the pastoral situation was to insist that the shepherds were rulers of sheep and so compare them to politicians or bishops or what not; this piled the heroic convention onto the pastoral one since the hero was another symbol of his whole society. Such a pretense, no doubt, made the characters unreal, but not the feelings expressed or even the situation (as opposed to the setting) described. The same pretense is often valuable in modern writing.

Which of the following is LEAST likely to be found in a Renaissance pastoral?

(a) Serious intent
(b) The heroic convention
(c) Symbolism
(d) Elegance of expression
(e) Accurate depiction of social structures

In lines 14–16 the author finds it necessary to oppose the situation to the setting because

(a) in pastoral poetry a possibly real situation is conveyed by unreal characters in unreal scenes
(b) setting and situation are natural opposites
(c) the addition of the heroic convention makes the pastoral setting an absurd situation
(d) situation and setting are the same in modern writing
(e) in pastoral poetry the pretense makes the setting even more real than the situation

The author would say that of the following the LEAST artificial element in pastoral poetry is the

(a) heroic convention
(b) characterization
(c) level of language
(d) underlying emotion
(e) pastoral convention

Record your stopping time: Hour _____ Minute _____ Second _____

Source: Adapted from *Principles of Educational and Psychological Testing*, second edition, by Frederick G. Brown. Copyright © 1970 by the Dryden Press Inc. Copyright © by Holt, Rinehart and Winston. Reprinted by permission of Holt, Rinehart and Winston.

Answers: (E), (A), and (D).

Box 2.1 A Reading Comprehension Test

allows her to perform well on mathematical tasks. Again, these problems are at the core of the ability problem.

Finally, suppose you were a school teacher interested in individualizing instruction for your students. In order to be a more effective teacher it would be useful if you knew something about the abilities each student is bringing to your class. How do you find out what a student's abilities or experiences are? In general, this problem has been solved by administering standardized tests to children and then translating their performance into scores for each measured ability. But as a skeptical teacher you might not be satisfied with a list of test scores for various nebulous ability categories. Such information is not very specific and does not really pinpoint what a child's capabilities are. They are, instead, very gross measures. You might therefore ask, what are the particular features of my student's cognitive system that permit a good performance in tests of one ability but a poor performance in tests of another? Again, this is the ability problem, and this chapter will show how cognitive psychologists have attempted to deal with it.

THE TRADITIONAL APPROACH

Very early in the development of psychology, an important observation was made: People differ from one another. They differ in the way they react to certain situations, in the way they interact with other people, in the things they like and dislike, and so on. This observation led to the factor (or trait) theory of human behavior—the idea that certain definable factors or traits underlie human behavior and that each person can be described as scoring at some level on each trait. This was not a particularly novel idea, since philosophers had dealt with the problem of traits for centuries. However, psychologists developed a field called psychometrics to answer the questions of (1) what are the major traits and (2) how can they best be measured? Thus, what had once been a philosophical question turned out to be a problem of how to develop testing techniques.

The first breakthrough came near the turn of this century when Alfred Binet was asked to design a test that would predict success in French schools (see Wolf, 1973). Binet's method of measuring intellectual ability was quite straightforward. First, he selected test items that involved common tasks that children of a given age group could perform, such as reciting the days of the week or making change (see Box 2.2). He then determined which tasks could be performed by the average child in each age group. Next, in order to measure the intellectual ability of a child, Binet noted whether or not the child was able to succeed on tasks that other children of that age group could succeed on; if the child could not, then the score would be below average; but if the child could go on and perform tasks that older children knew then the score would be above average. Finally, the test scores were compared to actual academic performance (such as grades). Test items that were not predictive of school success were dropped from the tests. Binet's test was so successful in predicting school performance that by the 1920s it became the basis for intelligence tests used in America and around the world. Thus, it is clear that from the beginning the measurement of intellectual ability has been validated by comparing test scores to success in schools.

Binet's work showed that it was possible to produce instruments for measuring important abilities. The psychometric (or testing) field of psychology now needed to face the issue of determining the major human traits. In order to solve this problem, new statistical tools were developed that freed psychology from the rhetoric of philosophy and allowed a means of determining the key factors underlying intellectual performance. One of the major statistical inventions was called factor analysis. The general procedure was to give a large number of different types of tests to a large group of people. Then factor analysis techniques were used to determine which tests seemed to be related to one another. For example, if people who scored high on test A also scored high on test B (and people who scored low on test A also scored low on test B, and so on), it could be concluded that test A and test B were really measuring the same single factor.

Spearman (1904; 1927) used factor analysis techniques to show that all tests of intellectual ability were related to one another, although not perfectly. In other words, if you scored high on one you would be likely to score high on others. Thus Spearman pro-

Age two

1. Three-hole Form Board. Placing three geometric objects in form board.
2. Delayed Response. Identifying placement of hidden object after 10-second delay.
3. Identifying Parts of the Body. Pointing out features on paper doll.
4. Block Building Tower. Building four-block tower by imitating examiner's procedure.
5. Picture Vocabulary. Naming common objects from pictures.
6. Word Combinations. Spontaneous combination of two words.

Age six

1. Vocabulary. Correctly defining 6 words on 45-word list.
2. Differences. Telling difference between two objects.
3. Mutilated Pictures. Pointing out missing part of pictured object.
4. Number Concepts. Counting number of blocks in a pile.
5. Opposite Analogies II. Items of form "Summer is hot; winter is _____."
6. Maze Tracing. Finding shortest path in simple maze.

Age ten

1. Vocabulary. Correctly defining 11 words on same list.
2. Block Counting. Counting number of cubes in three-dimensional picture, some cubes hidden.
3. Abstract Words I. Definition of abstract adverbs.
4. Finding Reasons I. Giving reasons for laws or preferences.
5. Word Naming. Naming as many words as possible in one minute.
6. Repeating Six Digits. Repeating six digits in order.

Average adult

1. Vocabulary. Correctly defining 20 words.
2. Ingenuity I. Algebraic word problems involving mental manipulation of volumes.
3. Differences between Abstract Words. Differentiating between two related abstract words.
4. Arithmetical Reasoning. Word problems involving simple computations.
5. Proverbs I. Giving meaning of proverbs.
6. Orientation: Direction II. Finding orientation after a verbal series of changes in directions.
7. Essential Differences. Giving principal difference between two related concepts.
8. Abstract Words III. Meanings of abstract adverbs.

Source: Adapted from *Principles of Educational and Psychological Testing,* second edition, by Frederick G. Brown. Copyright © 1970 by the Dryden Press Inc. Copyright © by Holt, Rinehart and Winston. Reprinted by permission of Holt, Rinehart and Winston.

Box 2.2   Typical Test Items on the Stanford–Binet Test

claimed the "two-factor theory" of intellectual ability—the idea that there is one factor for general intelligence (which he called g) and many smaller factors that are specific to individual tests (which he called s). Thus, your performance on a test was jointly determined by your general ability plus your specific abilities for the particular type of test.

Later, Thurstone (1938) modified the factor analysis technique and found that all tests of intellectual ability could be grouped into seven primary mental abilities: verbal comprehension, number, memory, perceptual speed, space, verbal fluency, and inductive reasoning. Thus, where Spearman found one primary ability (g), Thurstone found seven abilities worthy of measurement.

Finally, Guilford (1959; 1967) developed a system for specifying 120 separate mental abilities. His theory, called structure of the intellect, was not based on factor analysis but rather on a logical analysis of the factors involved in mental functioning. As shown in Box 2.3, he categorized all mental abilities within a framework consisting of three dimensions: the operations that are required in the task, the products of the mental operations, and the specific content of the problem. Since there are 5 operations, 6 products, and 4 contents, there are $5 \times 6 \times 4$ or 120 possible categories of mental abilities. Tests have been found that measure most of Guilford's 120 factors, but there are still no tests for several of them. Box 2.3 shows some examples of the tests corresponding to several factors in this system.

The theories of Spearman, Thurstone, and Guilford demonstrate the problems in locating the major human factors. However, if the psychometricians had trouble in defining factors, they certainly had less trouble in measuring a factor once it was defined. While there are many ways to define a good test, most psychometricians would include the following criteria:

Reliable. The test should result in the same score each time one person takes a version of it.

Valid. The test should measure what it says it is measuring. For example, a test of general intelligence should be able to predict school success.

Objective. The test should be easy to score and should result in the same score regardless of who scores it.

Structure of the Intellect

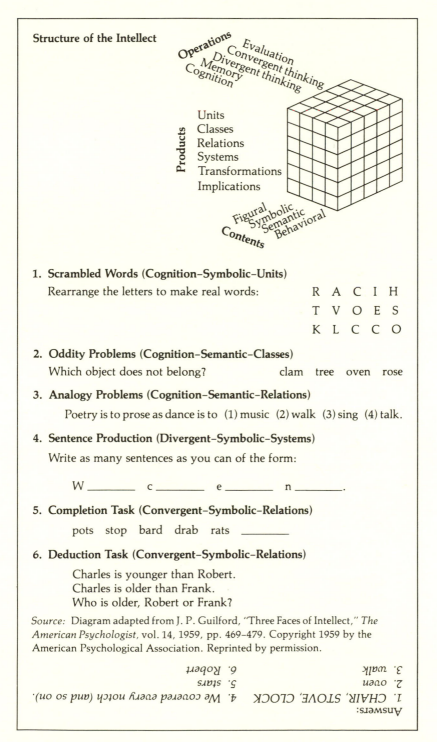

Operations
Evaluation
Convergent thinking
Divergent thinking
Memory
Cognition

Products
Units
Classes
Relations
Systems
Transformations
Implications

Figural
Symbolic
Semantic
Behavioral
Contents

1. **Scrambled Words (Cognition–Symbolic–Units)**

   Rearrange the letters to make real words:

   R A C I H

   T V O E S

   K L C C O

2. **Oddity Problems (Cognition–Semantic–Classes)**

   Which object does not belong?   clam   tree   oven   rose

3. **Analogy Problems (Cognition–Semantic–Relations)**

   Poetry is to prose as dance is to (1) music (2) walk (3) sing (4) talk.

4. **Sentence Production (Divergent–Symbolic–Systems)**

   Write as many sentences as you can of the form:

   W _____ c _____ e _____ n _____ .

5. **Completion Task (Convergent–Symbolic–Relations)**

   pots   stop   bard   drab   rats   _____

6. **Deduction Task (Convergent–Symbolic–Relations)**

   Charles is younger than Robert.
   Charles is older than Frank.
   Who is older, Robert or Frank?

Source: Diagram adapted from J. P. Guilford, "Three Faces of Intellect," *The American Psychologist*, vol. 14, 1959, pp. 469–479. Copyright 1959 by the American Psychological Association. Reprinted by permission.

Answers:

1. CHAIR, STOVE, CLOCK   2. oven   3. walk

4. We covered every notch (and so on).   5. stars   6. Robert

Box 2.3 Guilford's 120 Mental Factors and Some Sample Test Items

1. Select test items.
2. Determine measurement standards.
3. Administer test to a large sample.
4. Compare test scores to real-world performance of sample. If test is highly predictive, stop. If some of the test items are not predictive, eliminate them and go back to step 1.

Box 2.4   Procedure for Developing a Test

Standard. The test should be given to a large population so that it is possible to tell where a given score stands compared to all others from that population.

Tests that are to varying degrees reliable, valid, objective, and standardized have been developed for many factors (see Buros, 1972, for a listing of existing tests).

The psychometric approach is a scientific approach to the ability problem outlined at the beginning of this chapter. In a sense, it is a self-correcting procedure. If you want a test that will distinguish between students who will do well in learning to read and those who will not, you develop a test, administer it to people, observe whether it predicts performance, change items in the test that don't predict, and so on. This procedure is summarized in Box 2.4. (Further information can be obtained from the Suggested Readings at the end of this chapter.)

By this point, it should be clear that the technology of testing is well established. However, there is something left unfulfilled by the accomplishments of the psychometric approach. The psychometricians were much better at measuring factors than at defining them. For example, Box 2.5 shows that a person's response to a stimulus situation is supposed to be determined by scores for one or more relevant factors; for verbal ability, the relevant factors underlying performance are the ability to use proper grammar, the ability to spell, the ability to retain information from a short passage, and the ability to recognize definitions of words. As you can see, there was not much theoretical work aimed at describing *why* someone who scored high on a certain test would probably

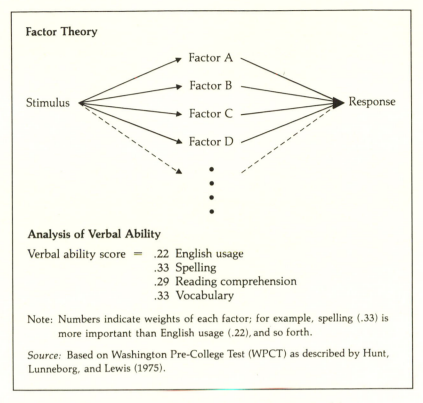

Factor Theory

Stimulus → Factor A, Factor B, Factor C, Factor D → Response

Analysis of Verbal Ability

Verbal ability score = .22 English usage
.33 Spelling
.29 Reading comprehension
.33 Vocabulary

Note: Numbers indicate weights of each factor; for example, spelling (.33) is more important than English usage (.22), and so forth.

Source: Based on Washington Pre-College Test (WPCT) as described by Hunt, Lunneborg, and Lewis (1975).

Box 2.5   Psychometric Approach to the Ability Problem

do well in some future task. The statistical tools allowed the development of measurement instruments, but it was not until the last ten years or so that the tools of cognitive psychology have been applied to the issue of what ability tests measure.

THE COGNITIVE APPROACH

The psychometric approach succeeded in its goals of locating and measuring traits, but it did not really tell us as much as we would like to know about the mechanisms underlying them. The psychometric approach never really developed a strong theoretical basis; it was, apparently, easier to measure abilities than to define or understand them. This is where cognitive psychology can help.

The cognitive tool that is most useful for solving the ability problem is the general information processing model. The main idea is that all humans come equipped with the same basic information processing system (IPS), as shown in Box 2.6. The main components of the information processing system are:

Short-term sensory store (STSS). Information coming in from the outside world impinges on our sense receptors. It is first held in an STSS (also called a sensory buffer by some theorists). This store holds information in its raw physical form exactly as presented. It can hold everything that was presented (unlimited capacity), but information fades very rapidly (rapid time decay). There may be a different STSS for each sense. For example, the STSS for visual information can be thought of as a snapshot that is exact, complete, and fades within a half second.

Short-term memory (STM). If attention is paid to the information in STSS before it fades away, some of it may be transferred to STM. This store may convert the raw sensory information into another modality, such as changing visually presented letters into sounds. The holding capacity of STM is limited to about seven items (limited capacity), although clever chunking techniques can increase the power of STM. Items are lost from STM when they are bumped out by new incoming items or when they are not actively rehearsed. STM can be thought of as conscious memory—it holds all that a person can be aware of at one time.

Working memory (WM). Many theorists add an appendage to short-term memory called working memory or intermediate term memory. Like STM, this memory has limited capacity, stores information in a form other than raw sensation, and forgets due to overloading or failure to rehearse. You can think of working memory as a scratch pad on which you perform conscious mental operations such as mental arithmetic.

Long-term memory (LTM). If information is held in short-term memory, there are encoding processes that allow it to be transferred to long-term memory. Long-term memory, like STSS, is unlimited in capacity, so it can hold vast amounts of information. But unlike STSS, LTM does not fade with time; however, items are lost because new information blocks the routes for retrieval of information from LTM. You can think of LTM as an organized storehouse of information, in which each item must be found by following a search path.

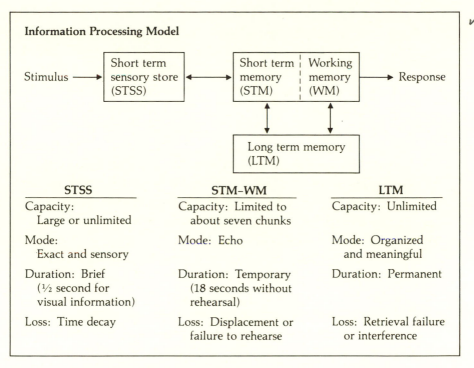

Box 2.6 Cognitive Approach to Ability Problem

Some of the main control processes in the information processing system are

Attention. Transferring information from STSS to STM.

Rehearsal. Keeping information active in consciousness in STM or WM.

Chunking. Techniques for clustering information in STM.

Operations in WM. Manipulating information in working memory.

Encoding. Transferring information from STM to LTM.

Searching LTM. Finding a target item in LTM.

The components and processes discussed above and illustrated in Box 2.6 represent a typical description of the information processing system, although different theorists may use slightly different arrangements. It is beyond the scope of this book to

document the case for the existence of each component and process listed above, but this chapter will attempt to show how this
model can be applied to problems in psychology. (See Lindsay
and Norman, 1977, for a discussion of the IPS.)

Let's assume that all humans possess the same general IPS
system consisting of STSS, STM, LTM, attention processes for
getting information from STSS to STM, rehearsal and chunking
processes for holding information in STM, encoding processes for
getting information from STM to LTM, and search processes for
finding a target in LTM. However, let's suppose that humans
differ with respect to the character and size of each memory store
and control process. For example, some people may be faster in
searching LTM than other people; some people may be able to
hold more information in STM at a time than other people; some
people may have better attentional strategies for getting information into STM before it fades away; and so on.

As an example, let's consider some of the differences that might
be important for reading and verbal processing. For example, the
speed with which one can find a target in long-term memory is
important, since the decoding of letters and words requires such a
search. Hunt, Lunneborg, and Lewis (1975) point out there are
500,000 morphemes (the building blocks of meaning) in a typical
pocket novel. Thus a major part of reading is looking up each
important word or letter group in memory to find its decoded
meaning. Even if people are very fast in recognizing morphemes,
a slight difference in search time would result in considerable differences in reading speed when it is multiplied by half a million.

Another important component of the IPS that may be involved
in reading involves the holding capacity of short-term memory.
How much can be held in STM at one time? If a person can hold
many words at once, without mixing up the order, then the task of
reading should be a bit easier. Even a small difference in capacity
would be magnified greatly when you consider how many times
STM must be filled at the rate of a few words per cycle. Differences in the holding capacity of STM would be especially important when long, complicated sentences are used.

Finally, another important component of the IPS that may be

involved in reading is the speed with which operations can be performed on verbal information in STM. For example, in reading
one must keep the words in order and decide which one is the
subject, object, predicate, and so on. If mental operations in STM
require even slightly more time for some people as compared to
others, this difference could show up as a large difference in
overall comprehension and reading ability. These components are
summarized in Box 2.7.

There are, of course, many other features of the information
system that may differ from person to person; examples include
the tendency to use verbal versus visual rehearsal mechanisms,
the organization strategy of LTM, the speed with which STSS
fades, and so on. The main idea here is that differences on tests of
ability—such as verbal ability—can be analyzed into differences
in the characteristics of people's information processing systems.
The next section provides examples of this technique.

EXAMPLES OF THE COGNITIVE APPROACH

Earl Hunt and his colleagues (Hunt, 1976; Hunt, 1978; Hunt,
Frost, and Lunneborg, 1973; Hunt and Lansman, 1975; Hunt,
Lunneborg, and Lewis, 1975) have successfully applied the cognitive tool described in the previous section to the problem of
individual differences. The cognitive tool is the analysis of ability
in terms of the components in the information processing system
(IPS); that is, in terms of the memory stores and processes that
are involved in performing a given task. In particular, Hunt took
a group of college freshmen who scored high in verbal ability and
a group who scored low in verbal ability as measured by a standardized college entrance exam (like the SAT). He then set out to
answer the question, what are the differences between these two
groups in terms of their information processing systems?

Decoding Processes in Long-Term Memory

One important component of the IPS that may be relevant to
verbal ability is the speed with which a person can search through

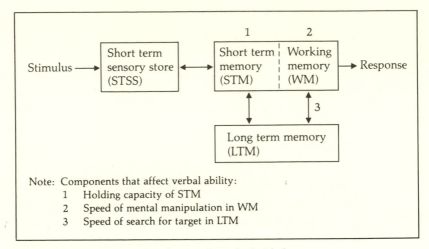

Note: Components that affect verbal ability:
  1   Holding capacity of STM
  2   Speed of mental manipulation in WM
  3   Speed of search for target in LTM

Box 2.7   Cognitive Analysis of Verbal Ability

long-term memory for a particular well-learned piece of information. For example, one very simple decoding process is to
recognize a single letter. In reading and verbal comprehension,
part of the task is simply to decode the printed letters into an
internal representation. A person must be able to look at a printed
letter and find its meaning in long-term memory.

How can you measure this simple cognitive process of letter
recognition? Fortunately for Hunt, a test of decoding processes in
long-term memory had already been developed by Posner, Boies,
Eichelman, and Taylor (1969). The general procedure is to present
the subject with two letters on a screen—such as Aa—and ask the
subject to press a *yes* (same) or *no* (different) button. As shown in
Box 2.8, there are two separate tasks. In the physical match task
the subject presses the *yes* button if both letters are identical, but
no if they are not (AA is *yes*, Aa is *no*); in the name match task
the subject presses the *yes* button if both letters have the same
name and the *no* button if not (Aa or AA are *yes*; AB is *no*).

What cognitive processes are involved in each task? For the
physical match task the subject must get the stimuli into STM,
make a decision, and then execute a response; for the name match
task the subject must get the stimuli into STM, look up the name
for each letter in LTM, make a decision, and then execute a

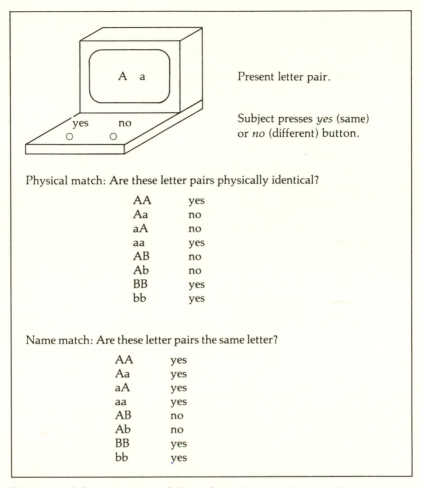

Present letter pair.

Subject presses *yes* (same) or *no* (different) button.

Physical match: Are these letter pairs physically identical?

AA	yes
Aa	no
aA	no
aa	yes
AB	no
Ab	no
BB	yes
bb	yes

Name match: Are these letter pairs the same letter?

AA	yes
Aa	yes
aA	yes
aa	yes
AB	no
Ab	no
BB	yes
bb	yes

Box 2.8   Measurement of Decoding Process Using a Posner Task

response. Thus, the two tasks involve the same processes except that the name match task contains one additional step—searching long-term memory for the names of the two letters. This step is not necessary for the physical match task since it is not necessary to figure out the names of the letters. Thus by using a subtraction technique we can say that the time to look up the name for the letters in LTM equals the time for a name match minus the time for a physical match. Since reading involves many instances of looking up letter names (and morpheme names) in long-term memory, Hunt predicted that he could find a difference on this skill between high and low verbal students.

To test this prediction, Hunt gave a modified version of the physical match test and the name match test to a group of high verbal and a group of low verbal subjects. Their average time to make a physical match was about the same, indicating that the groups did not differ much in how fast they could get letters into STM, make decisions, or execute responses. However, the low verbal group required much more time than the high verbal subjects when performing on the name match test. In one experiment, the difference between the time for a name match and time for a physical match was 33 milliseconds for the high verbal group and 86 milliseconds for the low verbal group. In another experiment, the differences were 64 milliseconds for the high verbal and 89 milliseconds for the low verbal. These results show that the decoding process of finding a name for a letter in long-term memory takes more time for low verbal than for high verbal subjects. Admittedly, the low verbals are just a fraction of a second slower (25 to 50 milliseconds); however, this decoding process must be repeated over and over thousands of times in the course of reading a single passage.

What can be concluded from this IPS analysis of verbal ability? One important implication is that gross differences in verbal ability may be describable in more detail. Note that low verbal students are not slower in getting information into STM and in executing a response (as required in the physical match task). However, low verbal students are consistently slower in searching LTM for a well-known target (as required in the name match task).

Holding Capacity of Short-Term Memory

As verbal information comes into short-term memory, it must be held there momentarily while decoding processes and other comprehension processes are carried out. In reading you must be able to hold the last few letters in memory so that you can later put them together to make a word, or you must be able to hold the last few words in memory so that you can later put them together into a clause. If the holding capacity of short-term memory is small then the process of comprehension will require more work and be subject to more error.

How can you measure the holding capacity of short-term memory? Again, Hunt and his colleagues were fortunate because cognitive psychologists had already developed techniques for measuring the capacity of short-term memory. They used a modified version of a task developed by Peterson and Peterson (1959). In Hunt's version of the task, subjects were presented with four letters on a screen one at a time; then there was a distractor task of reading numbers from the screen for a few seconds; and then subjects were asked to recall the four letters in order (see Box 2.9). This task requires that the person hold information in short-term memory while concentrating on something else. Similarly, reading involves taking in stimuli and holding them in memory for a few seconds while taking in some more.

Hunt gave this recall task to high and low verbal subjects. The results were that the low verbal subjects made more errors on the task than high verbal students; for example, when the retention interval was short, the low verbal students made three times as many errors in recall. Thus the high ability subjects were able to retain the letters in order much better than the low ability subjects. This suggests that the high verbal students have a larger holding capacity for verbal stimuli in short-term memory.

Again, we have been able to describe the difference between high and low verbal students in terms of the differences in their information processing systems.

Manipulation of Information in Short-Term Memory

So far, we have looked at the speed of decoding letter names in long-term memory and the size of short-term memory. Another important IPS process that is crucial for verbal comprehension is the ability to perform rapid operations on the information held in short-term memory. In order to read, a person needs to be able to put letters together into words, words together into clauses, and so on.

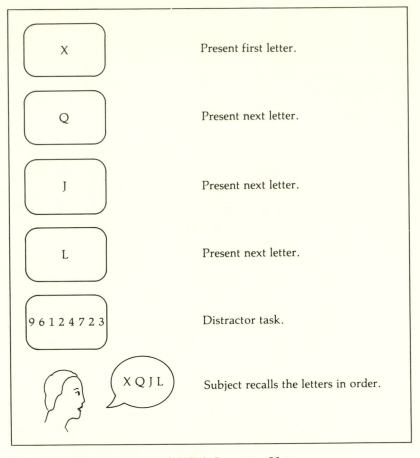

Box 2.9   Measurement of STM Capacity Using a
Modified Peterson Task

Again, when Hunt sought to measure the speed with which people can operate on information in short-term memory he found that cognitive psychologists had already developed some tests to help him. For example, he modified a task developed by Sternberg (1969) to produce the following test: The subject is presented with from one to five target letters, one at a time, for about 1 second each; then a probe letter is shown and the subject must press a *yes* button if the probe is the same as any of the target letters and a *no* if it is not (see Box 2.10).

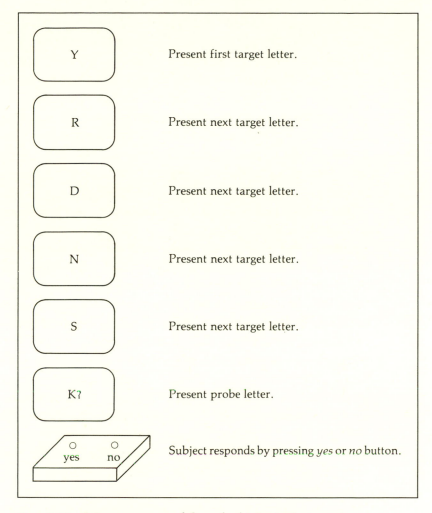

Y	Present first target letter.
R	Present next target letter.
D	Present next target letter.
N	Present next target letter.
S	Present next target letter.
K?	Present probe letter.
yes no	Subject responds by pressing *yes* or *no* button.

Box 2.10   Measurement of Speed of Manipulation of
Information in Working Memory Using a
Modified Sternberg Task

What is involved in this task when there is one target letter and
one probe? The subject must get the target into short-term memory, hold it there, get the probe letter into short-term memory,
make one mental comparison, and execute the response. When
there are two targets everything is the same except that two

mental comparisons are made instead of one; the probe is compared to the first letter and to the second letter. When there are
three targets there is one more mental comparison, and so on.
Thus we can look at the time added by adding one more target to
the task by using the following formula: The time to make a mental comparison equals the time to respond when there are n target
letters minus the time to respond when there are $n-1$ target
letters. Thus the Sternberg task provides a way of measuring the
time it takes to make one simple mental operation in working
memory.

The results again produced an interesting difference between
low and high ability subjects. The reaction time for the one-target
problems was at about the same level for both groups, but for
each added letter in the target (two-target, three-target, and so
on) there were about 80 milliseconds added to the time for low
verbal students and only 60 milliseconds added for high verbal
students. This difference in the slope of the response time curve
means that the time to make a mental operation in short-term
memory was considerably less for the high verbal students. In
other experiments, more complex mental operations were required and the same results were obtained; the time required for
each additional operation was more for the low verbal than for
the high verbal students. These results again show that it is possible to describe differences in verbal ability in terms of differences in people's information processing systems.

It is important to note that high verbal people do not perform
better on all tasks; rather, they excel on certain measures of relevant processing speeds and memory storage capacities. For example, low verbal people were not slower overall on tasks requiring
mainly reading a stimulus and executing a response. However,
when we increase the processing required in the task—such as
increasing the number of mental operations involved—then differences between high and low verbal people emerge.

• • •

The work of Hunt and his colleagues demonstrates how the IPS
model can make sense out of the long-standing problem of indi-

vidual differences in mental ability. Hunt's work provides some reason to believe that gross measures like tests of verbal ability, mathematical ability, or general intelligence may ultimately be understood in terms of differences in very simple cognitive stores and processes. For example, the difference between high and low verbal students seems to include differences in the search speed through LTM, the holding capacity of STM, and the speed of mental operations in STM. These are processes that seem to be fundamental building blocks in reading, processes that would be used over many times in the course of reading a passage. However, Hunt's work also demonstrates that many measures are not important in distinguishing between high and low verbal students; for example, general speed on executing a response is not related to the differences.

APPLYING WHAT YOU'VE LEARNED

So far, we have shown that the IPS model can be used as a way of solving the ability problem when the ability factor is verbal. Now, try to apply this knowledge to a different type of ability. For example, what are the components of the IPS that would be useful for becoming a good piano player? Take a moment and try to generate a list of two or three basic cognitive processes that might be useful in distinguishing a group of excellent piano players from those who are not able to learn piano very well. To start with, you might try to think of some ways of modifying the tasks that were discussed above. Which of the following tasks do you think would be important in characterizing good piano players?

Decoding of tones in long-term memory. First, subjects learn the names for eight different tones. Then, we can use a modified version of the physical and name match tasks. For the physical match we could present two tones and ask the subject to press a *yes* button if they were the same and a *no* button if they were different. For a name match we could present a tone and a name and again ask for a button-pressing response. In the name match task, however, the subject must locate the name of the tone by searching long-term memory. Thus we would measure the decoding time for recognizing a tone as follows: The time to find the name for a tone in LTM equals the time for a name match minus the time for a physical match. Would you predict that the speed of decoding tones would be faster for good piano players?

Holding capacity of short-term memory for tones. First, subjects learn to make eight different tones by pressing one of eight different keys. Then, we can use a modified version of the Peterson and Peterson task. Subjects listen to four tones presented in order, then there is a brief distracting task, then the subject tries to recreate the four tones by pressing four keys in order. Would you expect fewer errors in recall for the good piano players?

Manipulation of tones information in short-term memory. Finally, we can modify the Sternberg task so that the stimuli are tones. A subject listens to a series of from one to five target tones, then a probe tone is given. The subject presses a *yes* button if the probe is the same as any of the targets and a *no* if it is not. The additional time required for each additional tone gives a measure of the time to make a mental operation on tones in short-term memory. Do you predict differences in measure for good and poor piano players?

Can you now think of any other components in the IPS that might be relevant? If you wanted to test your predictions, how would you do it? One method would be to take a group of students who are all beginning piano lessons for the first time; test them with your cognitive tests; and then wait a year and see who are the successful students and who are the dropouts. Finally, compare the scores of the groups to see whether the dropouts have different IPS characteristics than the good piano learners.

FURTHER APPLICATIONS OF THE INFORMATION PROCESSING MODEL

In a recent symposium on "Intelligence Tests in the Year 2000" several participants were optimistic that tests of the future would be more closely tied to a cognitive analysis of the IPS. For example, Horn (1979) identified the following trends for future testing:

We will measure several basic cognitive processes, de-emphasize the concept of a single attribute of general intelligence, focus on adult tasks, and make more use of computers for testing and scoring. Resnick (1979) predicted that the new cognitive tests would fill important roles in schools, including a means of individualizing instruction. Based on the papers presented at the symposium, Detterman (1979, p. 295) concluded that "intelligence tests will have a very different appearance than they do today."

More recently, Pellegrino and Glaser (1979) have made a distinction between two related cognitive approaches to the ability problem. The "cognitive correlates" approach, such as the work of Hunt discussed earlier, specifies the information processing components that are different in high and low ability groups. The "cognitive components" approach analyzes a task into its parts and seeks to determine which parts of the task are the source of the difference between high and low performers. Recent work using the latter approach has been directed at analyzing the processes involved in common items on IQ tests. For example, a common item on an IQ test is an analogy problem such as:

Hand is to foot as finger is to _____ .

> (a) head
>
> (b) thumb
>
> (c) toe
>
> (d) inch

Sternberg (1977) analyzed this task into its information processing components and measured the time required to accomplish each of the subprocesses. Based on his testing of large numbers of subjects, he was able to locate the basic information processes that are most important in distinguishing high from low scorers on an IQ test. Thus, performance on an IQ test can be understood in terms of the speed with which a person performs certain basic cognitive processes.

Another typical IQ test item is a series completion such as

axbxcxd ___ ___ ___

Simon and Kotovsky (1963) have provided an analysis of this task into its information processing components. Further, Holtzman, Glaser, and Pellegrino (1976) have successfully instructed schoolchildren on some of the components of such a test item. Many of the other items on typical tests of intellectual ability are currently being analyzed into the basic cognitive processes that are required.

This chapter has given you a very brief example of how the cognitive revolution is affecting one of the oldest areas in psychology—the measurement and description of individual differences in mental ability. It has provided an example of how one of the tools of cognitive psychology—the IPS model—can be used to take a traditional problem in psychology and make sense out of it. In the not-too-distant future we might no longer say things like, "Tom is high in verbal ability." Instead, it might make more sense to say that "Tom scores high on alphanumeric search speed," or "Tom scores high on the holding capacity of his verbal short-term memory." Perhaps the whole mystique of ability in general and intelligence in particular will finally be laid to rest, and we will at last be able to solve the ability problem raised at the beginning of this chapter.

SUGGESTED READINGS

Hunt, E., C. Lunneborg, and J. Lewis. What does it mean to be high verbal? *Cognitive Psychology,* 1975, *7,* 194–227. Describes research project on analysis of verbal ability that is discussed in this chapter.

Intelligence, 1979, *3,* No. 3. This issue of the journal *Intelligence* gives an excellent summary of the current status of the cognitive analysis of ability.

Lindsay, P. H., and D. A. Norman. *Human information processing.* New York: Academic Press, 1977. A general introduction to psychology from the information processing point of view.

Resnick, L. B. *The nature of intelligence.* Hillsdale, N.J.: Erlbaum, 1976. Contains many important papers describing how cognitive psychologists are studying differences in intellectual abilities.

Sternberg, R. J. *Intelligence, information processing, and analogical reasoning: The Componential Analysis of Human Reasoning.* Hillsdale, N.J.: Erlbaum, 1977. Describes a research project aimed at analyzing the information processing components involved in solving verbal analogy problems.

3 Cognitive Process Models

THE PROCEDURAL SKILL PROBLEM

A major component of the early schooling of a child generally involves the learning of basic arithmetic skills such as the ability to add, subtract, multiply, and divide. Many students acquire these skills, although there is some appalling evidence that some do not. The main question raised in this chapter is, what knowledge does a person have when he or she is able to engage in some procedural skill? This question can be called the procedural skill problem. One aspect of the procedural skill problem concerns the acquisition of basic arithmetic skills. For example, consider the following subtraction problems:

$$\begin{array}{cccc} 763 & 792 & 806 & 890 \\ -541 & -668 & -577 & -722 \\ \hline \end{array}$$

Can you describe what someone who can solve these problems knows?

Another aspect of this question concerns the knowledge of a person who makes errors on a certain procedure. For example, look at Sheila's performance:

$$\begin{array}{cccc} 763 & 792 & 806 & 890 \\ -541 & -668 & -577 & -722 \\ \hline 222 & 136 & 371 & 172 \end{array}$$

Can you describe the procedure that Sheila is using?

Cognitive psychologists seek to answer these kind of questions by providing a detailed description of the procedure a person has acquired for a given task like subtraction. As this chapter will show, the tool that has been most successful in solving the procedural skill problem has been a technique for analyzing a cognitive process into its parts.

THE TRADITIONAL APPROACH

The traditional approach to the procedural skill problem was based on S–R association as put forth by E. L. Thorndike (1913, 1931) in the first third of this century. His description of learning arithmetic skills was quite straightforward: The child simply learns to make many stimulus–response associations. For example, the stimulus is the problem (for example, $5 + 5 =$ ____) and the response is the correct answer (10). The process of learning involves the formation of an association between an individual stimulus and its response.

Suppose that a child learns an arithmetic fact such as $8 - 5 = 3$. Box 3.1 shows how the traditional S–R approach might describe the learning process. At the start of learning, the stimulus $(8-5)$ may be associated with many possible answers in the child's memory; thus, a child may have a mild tendency to respond with 3, 2, 4, 13, or other numbers. Thorndike proposed several laws of learning to account for the acquisition of procedural skills. One such law, the law of exercise, included the idea that the association becomes stronger and stronger as the child practices more and more. Thus as the child recites "$8-5=3$" the association between the stimulus $(8-5)$ and the correct response (3) becomes stronger. Another important law, the law of effect, included the idea that feedback helps strengthen the association with the correct response and weaken associations with other responses. If incorrect responses such as 2 or 13 are punished by the teacher saying "try again," these responses become less strongly associated with the stimulus $(8-5)$. If the correct response is rewarded by the teacher saying "right," it becomes more strongly associated with the stimulus. According to this theory, the learning of basic arithmetic skills involves memorizing many separate S–R associations.

This approach to the learning of procedural skills made some

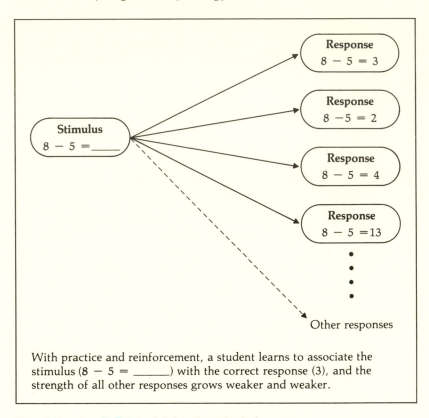

With practice and reinforcement, a student learns to associate the stimulus ($8 - 5 = $ _____) with the correct response (3), and the strength of all other responses grows weaker and weaker.

Box 3.1   An S–R Model for Simple Subtraction

sense to the psychologists and educators of Thorndike's time because it fit the existing theories and tools of psychology. However, consider how many rote pieces of information a student would have to learn according to this theory. For simple addition of one-digit numbers such as $2 + 2$ and $5 + 8$ there are 90 different problems; if we include two-digit numbers there are over 8000 different addition facts. Furthermore, the same figures apply in turn to subtraction, multiplication, and division. A person would need to memorize literally thousands of arithmetic facts, many of which are never or only rarely used.

According to Thorndike's S–R theory of procedural skill, the best way to learn arithmetic is to perform many problems repeatedly with feedback on each problem, which translates into rote drill and many tests. This approach led to some strong reactions, such as Brownell's (1935) assertion that learning arithmetic should be based on the child's understanding of underlying principles rather than on memorization of isolated facts. It should be noted that Thorndike's approach did have an impact on education, and certainly provided a reform over earlier practices. However, it has not been until fairly recently that psychologists could offer a theoretically useful alternative to Thorndike's S-R approach. Let us now turn to this alternative—the approach of modern cognitive psychology.

THE COGNITIVE APPROACH

The S-R approach emphasized the idea that a person acquires the correct behavior for each given stimulus situation. According to the cognitive approach, a person does not acquire behavior directly but rather acquires a higher-order procedure or rule system that can be used to generate behavior in many situations.

In order to attack the procedural skill problem, cognitive psychologists have had to develop rigorous tools for analyzing a cognitive process into its parts. They have successfully applied several techniques for formally analyzing and specifying the procedural knowledge that a person applies to a given problem. Two useful ways of representing procedural knowledge are to draw flowcharts or to write a program. A program is just a list of things to do that you start at the top and follow one step at a time. A flowchart is a set of boxes and arrows that describes the processes and decisions involved for some procedure. Let's explore each of these cognitive tools.

For example, let's suppose that you know an inventive five-year-old, Kenny, who is able to give correct answers for single-digit subtraction problems. As a good cognitive psychologist you might be interested in figuring out what cognitive procedure he uses to solve the problems. In order to get a better idea of Kenny's procedural knowledge about subtraction, you could interview him about his procedure, try to generate a flowchart or program that corresponds to his procedure, and test it by comparing its performance to that of the five-year-old.

Program for Counting Up Procedure

1. *Set counters.* (Set fingers to smaller number; set voice to zero.)
2. *Do fingers equal larger number?* If *yes,* stop and recite; if *no,* go on to step 3.
3. *Increment counters by 1.*
4. *Go back to step 2.*

Box 3.2   A Process Model for Simple Subtraction (Program Format)

The first thing to do, then, is to observe and interview our little friend carefully. When we watch him we see that he seems to be using his fingers and his voice to count. For example, if we give the problem "What is 8 take away 5?" he puts out 5 fingers, then 6 fingers and says "1," then 7 fingers and says "2," then 8 fingers and says "3," and finally he says, "The answer is 3." With a little more interviewing and questioning, we find that he has learned to subtract by using what he already knows about counting.

The next step is to look over the protocol of Kenny's subtraction behavior and try to describe it more precisely. Can you describe his procedure as a program? The procedure may be as follows:

1. *Set counters.* Your fingers serve as one counter and your voice serves as another. Put out the number of fingers corresponding to the lower number, and your voice will start out at zero.
2. *Do fingers equal larger number?* Does the number of fingers you have out equal the larger number? If so, stop and recite how many times you have incremented your finger counter. If not, go on to step 3.
3. *Increment counters by 1.* Put out one more finger and also recite by voice how many times you have come to step 3.
4. *Go back to step 2.*

This procedure is summarized in Box 3.2.

You can also represent this procedure as a flowchart as shown in Box 3.3. The diamond represents a decision (whether or not to

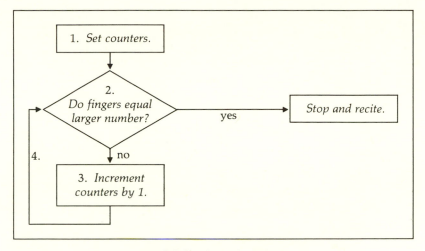

Box 3.3 A Process Model for Simple Subtraction
(Flowchart Format)

stop) and the rectangles represent processes (things to do). Can
you see that the flowchart and the program convey the same
information about the procedure for subtracting by counting?
These analyses of cognitive processes can be called process
models because they are models of what a person knows.

The next step is to test your representation of Kenny's subtraction procedure. You could compare Kenny's performance against
the performance of your representation of his procedure. The
model does not make any errors for single-digit subtraction, and
when we test Kenny we find that he makes no errors either. However, the model does suggest that some problems will be more difficult than others. For example, the more times that step 3 (count
aloud) has to be repeated, the more time the problem will take.

When we apply the model we have built to the 8 − 5 problem
we find the following: The finger counter is set to 5 (step 1), we
have not yet reached 8 so we go on (step 2), we add one finger and
say "1" (step 3), we return to step 2 and see that we still have not
reached 8, we add another finger giving us 7 and say "2" (step 3),
we return to step 2 and still do not have 8 fingers, we add another
finger now giving us 8 and say "3" (step 3), we go back to step 2,
and now we have 8 fingers so we stop and say "3." This solution

---

1. Put out 5 fingers.
2. Number of fingers is not 8 so go on.
3. Put out one more finger (6) and say "1."
4. Go on to step 2.
2. Number of fingers (6) is not 8 so go on.
3. Put out one more finger (7) and say "2."
4. Go on to step 2.
2. Number of fingers (7) is not 8 so go on.
3. Put out one more finger (8) and say "3."
4. Go on to step 2.
2. Number of fingers is 8 so stop and say "3."

Box 3.4   Performance of Process Model for $8 - 5 =$ _____

procedure is summarized in Box 3.4. The $8 - 5$ problem requires that we go through step 3 a total of three times; $8 - 6$ requires only two cycles through, and $8 - 7$ and $9 - 8$ require only one. If we compare predictions like these to Kenny's speed of solution we can test the accuracy of our model. If Kenny's solution times are longer for the problems that require many cycles (like $8 - 5$) but shorter for problems that require few cycles (like $8 - 7$), then we can say our model fits Kenny's performance. Box 3.5 graphs the model's performance against that of a human.

Resnick and her colleagues (Resnick, 1976b; Woods, Resnick, and Groen, 1975) have developed five simple models like the one described above and found that the performances of school children can be fit to one of them. Younger children tend to use procedures that are not totally efficient (like the model described above), but older children use highly efficient ones. Since these techniques are rarely taught explicitly, it seems that children are able to invent procedures and to revise them with experience. An important implication of Resnick's work is that different children may be giving the same answers for problems and yet be using entirely different procedures for generating them. Thus, instead of focusing on whether or not the child gives the correct answer for each problem (as suggested by S–R associationism), it is useful to focus on which procedure the child is using.

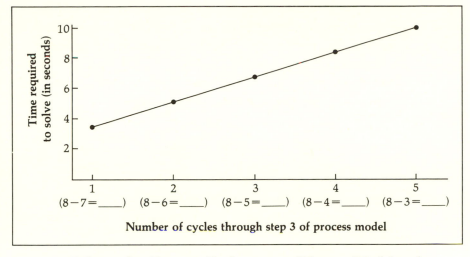

Box 3.5   Relationship Between Performance of Process Model and Performance of Human

The use of cognitive tools for solving the procedural knowledge problem is an important advance over the traditional approach to arithmetic learning. If we were using an S–R behaviorist approach we would say that when we give Kenny a problem like 8 − 5, he pauses, mumbles, moves his fingers, and says "3." We would not really have a good understanding of what was generating this behavior. However, instead of saying that a child has acquired the correct behavior or has not acquired the correct behavior, it is now possible using the cognitive approach to give a more precise description of the cognitive mechanism that a child uses to generate his or her behavior. Let's now see how this technique can be applied to the learning of other arithmetic skills.

EXAMPLES OF THE COGNITIVE APPROACH

Brown and Burton (1978) have shown how the cognitive process analysis techniques described in the previous section can be applied to the study of the real performance of children on arithmetic problems. In particular, they analyzed the procedure that one must know in order to solve subtraction problems correctly.

Also, they developed a list of bugs that children may incorporate into their own particular procedures, creating procedures that are similar to the correct one but have one or more components that are different.

First, let's try to analyze the procedure involved in subtraction of three-digit numbers such as the following:

$$\begin{array}{r} 763 \\ -541 \\ \hline 222 \end{array} \qquad \begin{array}{r} 792 \\ -668 \\ \hline 124 \end{array} \qquad \begin{array}{r} 806 \\ -577 \\ \hline 229 \end{array} \qquad \begin{array}{r} 890 \\ -722 \\ \hline 168 \end{array}$$

What are the processes and decisions involved in solving these kinds of problems? A step-by-step program for the correct procedure is given below.

1. *Set up problem.* First, you need to recognize the elements in the problem. You need to determine which digit belongs to the units space on top, the tens space on top, the hundreds space on top, the units space on bottom, the tens space on bottom, and the hundreds space on bottom. You can assume there is an erasable scoreboard with 9 spaces that looks something like this:

   $$\begin{array}{ccc} T(\text{hundreds}) = \underline{\quad} & T(\text{tens}) = \underline{\quad} & T(\text{units}) = \underline{\quad} \\ - \; B(\text{hundreds}) = \underline{\quad} & B(\text{tens}) = \underline{\quad} & B(\text{units}) = \underline{\quad} \\ \hline A(\text{hundreds}) = \underline{\quad} & A(\text{tens}) = \underline{\quad} & A(\text{units}) = \underline{\quad} \end{array}$$

   Each space has a name and a number is stored in that space. Once you have set up the problem you need to recognize that it is a subtraction problem and that you will start at the right, in the units column.

2. *Initiate subtraction procedure.* Now, you may begin the subtraction process, which consists of the following.

   2a. *Find $T - B$.* You must find the number at the top and the number at the bottom for the column you are working on. This involves simply looking in the spaces for the two numbers you need and setting them up as a subtraction problem.

   2b. *Is $T < B$?* Next you need to see whether or not you need to borrow. If the top number is less than the bottom number, you need to jump to the borrow procedure in step 3. If not, you can go on in this procedure to step 2c.

2c. *Subtract and write.* Since the top number is greater than or equal to the bottom number, just generate the answer to this problem and write it in the appropriate space for the column you are working on.

2d. *Continue?* If there are more columns to the left, go on and repeat the subtraction procedure starting at step 2a; otherwise, stop.

3. *Borrowing procedure.* You use this procedure only if you have determined (in step 2b) that you need to borrow.

3a. *Find next T.* First, you check the top number in the column to the left of the one you are working to see if you can borrow.

3b. *Is next T = 0?* If the number in the borrow column is equal to zero, you cannot borrow from it so you need to go to the *Borrowing from zero procedure* in step 4; if it is greater than zero, then you can use this borrow procedure and go on to step 3c.

3c. *Add 10.* Add 10 to the top number in the column you are working on, and write that number in the *T* space.

3d. *Subtract 1.* Subtract 1 from the top number in the column next to the one you are working on, and write that number in the *T* space in the borrow column.

3e. *Go to step 2.* You are now ready to carry out the subtraction procedure, so jump back to step 2 and continue from there.

4. *Borrowing from zero procedure.* Use this procedure only if you have determined (in step 3b) that you need to subtract from zero.

4a. *Find next T.* First, you need to check the top number that is two columns to the left of where you are working.

4b. *Is next T = 0?* If it is also zero, you need to jump to another procedure (not specified); otherwise, you can continue to step 4c.

4c. *Subtract 1.* Subtract 1 from the top number that is two columns to the left and write that number in its space.

4d. *Add 9.* Add 9 to the top number that is in the first column to the left, which contained a zero. That space will now have a 9 in it, so write 9 there.

---

1. *Set up problem*

2. *Initiate subtraction procedure.*

   2a. Find $T - B$.
   2b. Is $T < B$? If so go to step 3, otherwise go on.
   2c. Subtract and write and move to next column.
   2d. Continue? If there are more columns, repeat step 2a; otherwise, stop.

3. *Borrowing procedure.*

   3a. Find next T (from next column).
   3b. Is next $T = 0$? If so go to step 4, otherwise go on.
   3c. Add 10 to top number in current column.
   3d. Subtract 1 from top number in next left column.
   3e. Go to step 2.

4. *Borrowing from zero procedure.*

   4a. Find next T (from next column).
   4b. Is next $T = 0$? If so go to some new procedure, otherwise go on.
   4c. Subtract 1 from top number in second left column.
   4d. Add 9 to top number in left column.
   4e. Add 10 to top number in current column.
   4f. Go to step 2.

Box 3.6   A Process Model for Three-Digit Subtraction (Program Format)

4e. *Add 10.* Now, you can finally borrow the 10 you need for the column you are working on. Add 10 to the top number and write the new number in the space.

4f. *Go to step 2.* Now you are ready to proceed with the subtraction procedure, so go back to step 2.

As you can see we have written this subtraction procedure as a simple program; that is, as a list of things to do. You start at step 1 and work down; if you jump to a new line, you begin working down from there, ignoring any steps in between (see Box 3.6). We could also write it as a flowchart such as shown in Box 3.7. Note that decisions such as steps 2b, 3b, and 4b are indicated by diamonds, processes are indicated by rectangles, and the order of

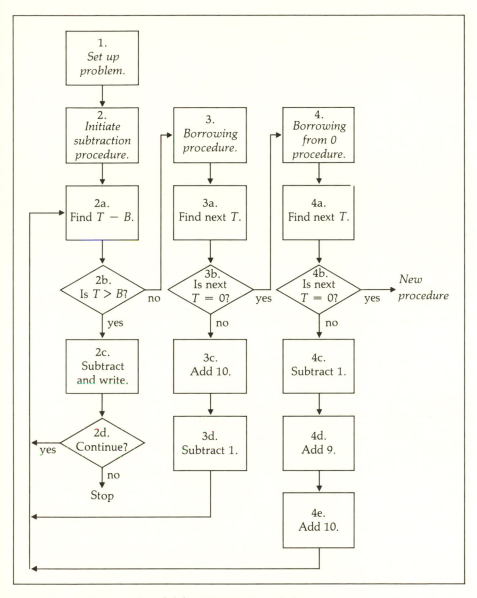

Box 3.7   A Process Model for Three-Digit Subtraction
   (Flowchart Format)

work is indicated by arrows. The flowchart in Box 3.7 and the
program in Box 3.6 are really saying the same thing. It is possible
to analyze a person's procedural knowledge using either method.

In order to make sure you understand this analysis of the cognitive processes for subtraction, let's try a problem:

$$846$$
$$-555$$

In step 1 we set up the problem as: T(hundreds) = 8, T(tens) = 4, T(units) = 6, B(hundreds) = 5, B(tens) = 5, B(units) = 5. We start in the right column and go to step 2a, where we find 6 − 5 = _____ as the first part of the problem. In step 2b we determine that no borrowing is needed, so we go on to step 2c, where we find the answer [A(units) = 1] and write it. Since there is another column (as determined in step 2d) we go to the tens column and start over. In step 2a we find 4 − 5 = _____. In step 2b we determine that borrowing is needed so we jump to step 3. The top number in the hundreds column is 8 (step 3a) so we determine that we can continue (step 3b). In step 3c we add 10 to the 4 in top tens column to get 14, and in step 3d we subtract 1 from the 8 in the hundreds column to get 7 there. We can now jump back to step 2a, and in step 2c we write the answer as 9 in the tens column. In step 2d we go to the hundreds column and start over. The last part of the problem is 7 − 5 = _____ (step 2a), which does not require borrowing (step 2b), so the answer is written as 2 in the hundreds column (step 2c) and we stop (step 2d). This process is summarized in Box 3.8.

So far we have looked at how to describe the procedural knowledge required in order to solve certain subtraction problems. However, let's suppose that a child has almost but not quite acquired this procedure; let's suppose that the child has one little bug in his or her procedure for subtraction. For example, what would happen if there were at bug a step 2b; instead of setting up each problem as taking the bottom number away from the top, the child sets up each problem as taking the smaller number away from the larger. In other respects, though, the child's procedure is correct. What answers would this child give for the following problems? (222, 136, 371, 172)

763	792	806	890
−541	−668	−577	−722

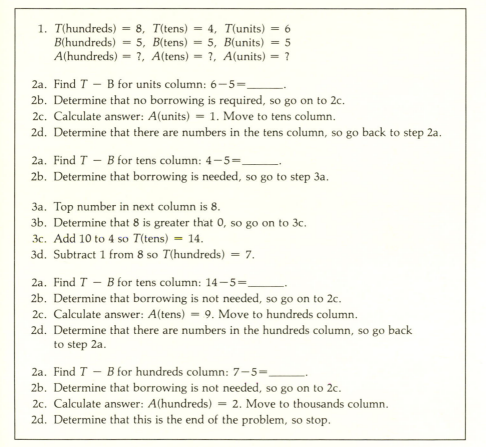

1. $T(\text{hundreds}) = 8$, $T(\text{tens}) = 4$, $T(\text{units}) = 6$
   $B(\text{hundreds}) = 5$, $B(\text{tens}) = 5$, $B(\text{units}) = 5$
   $A(\text{hundreds}) = ?$, $A(\text{tens}) = ?$, $A(\text{units}) = ?$

2a. Find $T - B$ for units column: $6-5=$_____.
2b. Determine that no borrowing is required, so go on to 2c.
2c. Calculate answer: $A(\text{units}) = 1$. Move to tens column.
2d. Determine that there are numbers in the tens column, so go back to step 2a.

2a. Find $T - B$ for tens column: $4-5=$_____.
2b. Determine that borrowing is needed, so go to step 3a.

3a. Top number in next column is 8.
3b. Determine that 8 is greater that 0, so go on to 3c.
3c. Add 10 to 4 so $T(\text{tens}) = 14$.
3d. Subtract 1 from 8 so $T(\text{hundreds}) = 7$.

2a. Find $T - B$ for tens column: $14-5=$_____.
2b. Determine that borrowing is not needed, so go on to 2c.
2c. Calculate answer: $A(\text{tens}) = 9$. Move to hundreds column.
2d. Determine that there are numbers in the hundreds column, so go back to step 2a.

2a. Find $T - B$ for hundreds column: $7-5=$_____.
2b. Determine that borrowing is not needed, so go on to 2c.
2c. Calculate answer: $A(\text{hundreds}) = 2$. Move to thousands column.
2d. Determine that this is the end of the problem, so stop.

Box 3.8 Performance of Process Model on $846 - 555 =$ _____

Or suppose that the child had a bug at step 3d in the borrowing procedure. Instead of subtracting 1 from the borrow column the child simply ignores this step. What answers would this child give to the problems listed above? (222, 134, 329, 178)

Or suppose that the child had a bug at step 4c in the borrowing from zero procedure. Instead of subtracting 1 from the hundreds column, this step is ignored. However, the child retains steps 4d and 4e and all the others. What answers would the child give for the above problems? (222, 124, 329, 168)

As you can see there are many bugs that may be present in the subtraction procedure a child uses. In other words, there are many procedures a child might use that lead to correct answers on some problems but errors on others. A good teacher may be able to look at the test performance of a student and notice which bugs seem to be present in his or her subtraction program. However, it has not been until the last few years that cognitive psychologists could really offer much help.

Brown and Burton (1978) have developed a computer program that uses the cognitive tool of analyzing tasks into process components. They tried to determine all the major bugs that children sometimes have in their programs for subtraction. For example, a group of 1325 students was given a large number of subtraction problems. The mistakes made by each student were carefully studied, and some of the most common bugs found in children's knowledge of subtraction were the following:

1. *Borrowing from zero.* When borrowing from a column that has a zero on top, the student changes it to a 9 but does not subtract 1 from the number to the left. For example, 205 − 126 = 179.

2. *Subtracting smaller number from larger.* When it is necessary to subtract the bottom number in a column from the top number, the student instead subtracts the smaller number from the larger. For example, 205 − 126 = 121.

3. *Moving over zero.* When subtracting the bottom number from the top number and the top number is zero, the student writes the bottom number as the answer. When the student borrows from a column that has a zero on top, the student skips that column and borrows from the next one. For example, 205 − 126 = 29.

Brown and Burton's computer program, called BUGGY, can be used to diagnose students' errors in subtraction. The student sits down in front of a computer terminal and is presented with subtraction problems. The computer has in its memory all the possible wrong procedures (as well as the correct one) that a student could use and tries to find the one that best fits the answers the child gives. For example, if a student behaves like Sheila (see the beginning of this chapter), the computer will find that the number 2 bug (subtracting smaller number from larger) is the one in her procedure. Sometimes more than one bug might be involved and sometimes children are not consistent, so the task of the computer is really a difficult one. BUGGY was moderately successful in characterizing the procedural knowledge of the 1325 children who were tested: 12 percent made no or only one or two errors, 21 percent made errors that could be completely explained by one or two bugs, 53 percent made errors that could partly be explained by one or two bugs, and 16 percent made errors that could not be explained at all by the known bugs. Based on the pattern of errors, the computer prints out the most likely bug or bugs that account for the student's answer. Thus, instead of giving each child a score of how many answers were correct, the BUGGY program is able to tell the teacher (and student) exactly where the procedural bug is located.

The work of Brown and Burton (1978) in developing the BUGGY program gives an excellent example of how the analytic techniques of cognitive psychology can be successfully used. Notice that the main tool of cognitive psychology in this case is the analysis of a cognitive process (the subtraction procedure) into its parts.

APPLYING WHAT YOU'VE LEARNED

We have just seen how the analysis of cognitive processes can be applied to subtraction. Now let's try the same technique with simple addition of two-digit numbers. For example, consider the following kinds of problems:

$$
\begin{array}{ccccc}
22 & 74 & 56 & 24 & 29 \\
+23 & +25 & +57 & +82 & +12 \\
\end{array}
$$

First, solve these problems yourself, giving a running description of what you are doing. In generating your protocol try to describe each process and decision you go through. Next, based on your running description, try to determine what processes and decisions are involved in your addition procedure. Take a few minutes to make a list of the steps that you think are involved. Did your program contain the following steps? Can you fill in the details?

1. T(tens) = 2, T(units) = 9
   B(tens) = 1, B(units) = 2

2a. Find $T + B$ for units column: $9 + 2 = $_____.
2b. Determine that answer is greater than 10, so go to step 3a.

3a. Write answer for units: A(units) = 1.
3b. Determine that there are numbers in the tens column,
    so go on to 3c.
3c. Add 1 to top number in tens column so T(tens) = 3.

2a. Find $T + B$ for tens column: $3 + 1 = $ _____.
2b. Determine that answer is not greater than or equal to 10,
    so go on to 2c.
2c. Write answer for tens column: A(tens) = 4.
2d. Determine that it is time to stop. (Answer: 41.)

Box 3.9 Performance of Complete Process Model
on $29 + 12 = $ _____

1. *Set up problem.*
2. *Add procedure.*

   2a. Find $T + B$ for the column you are on.

   2b. Is $T + B \geq 10$? If so, go to *Carry procedure* (step 3);
   otherwise, go on to step 2c.

   2c. Calculate and write answer for $T + B$.

   2d. Continue? If there is more to do, go back to step 2a;
   otherwise, stop.

3. *Carry procedure.*

   3a. Write right digit as answer for this column.

   3b. Numbers in next column? If there are no numbers in the
   next column, go to step 4; otherwise go on to step 3c.

   3c. Add 1 to top number in next column.

   3d. Go back to step 2.

4. *Carry to zero procedure.*

   4a. Write 1 in next column for answer.

   4b. Stop.

1. $T(\text{tens}) = 2$, $T(\text{units}) = 9$
   $B(\text{tens}) = 1$, $B(\text{units}) = 2$

2a. Find $T + B$ for units column: $9 + 2 = $_____.
2c. Write answer in units column: $A(\text{units}) = 11$.
2a. Find $T + B$ for tens column: $2 + 1 = $_____.
2c. Write answer for tens column: $A(\text{tens}) = 3$.
2d. No more columns, so stop. (Answer: 311.)

Box 3.10 Performance of Incomplete Process Model
on $29 + 12 = $ _____

According to this procedure, which of the problems given above will be the most difficult and which will be the easiest? You could count the number of steps each problem takes to determine which takes the longest. Time yourself on each problem. Did your solution times correspond with the predictions of your model? In other words, did the problems that the model says have more steps take longer to solve?

If you were going to generate a BUGGY-like diagnostic system, what are some of the major bugs you would look for? For example, if a child gives answers like the following,

$$\begin{array}{ccccc} 22 & 74 & 56 & 24 & 29 \\ +23 & +25 & +57 & +82 & +12 \\ \hline 45 & 99 & 1013 & 106 & 311 \end{array}$$

which of the steps in the child's procedure are defective? The problem seems to be that the subject skips step 2b and never uses step 3 or 4. Thus, when the sum of two numbers is a two-digit number both numbers are written in the column for the answer. This procedure consists only of steps 1, 2, 2a, 2c, and 2d. It sometimes gives the correct answer (such as for the first, second, and fourth problems above) but often fails. See Boxes 3.9 and 3.10.

In summary, a cognitive analysis of performance using a process model gives more information about what a child knows than just a raw score of percent correct. The basic steps for constructing a process model are as follows: First, human subjects are interviewed and asked to describe how they solve certain problems; second, a process model is constructed, such as one using flowcharts or a program; third, the performance predictions of the model are compared to the performance of real human subjects to see if they match.

FURTHER APPLICATIONS OF PROCESS MODELS

This chapter has given one example of how the performance of children on arithmetic problems can be analyzed in terms of underlying procedural knowledge. Although this line of research is a relatively new one, it has already displayed some progress. For example, Groen and Parkman (1972) were able to analyze the adding behavior of first graders, and Resnick and her colleagues (Resnick, 1976b; Woods, Resnick, and Groen, 1975) were able to analyze the subtraction behavior of second and fourth graders. In both cases there was evidence that the type of procedure becomes more sophisticated as the child grows. Thus, learning can be viewed as the acquisition of more and more powerful procedures. One promising aspect of this work is that the progress of a child may someday be measured in terms of which algorithms have been acquired rather than how many number facts he or she knows.

A logical extension of this line of work is to try to teach explicitly the higher order procedures that are useful in a subject like arithmetic. If we view skill learning as the acquisition of a useful procedure, why not explicitly teach the procedure? Instead of relying on the student to discover the procedure through drill and practice on problems, why not tell the student exactly what you are trying to teach? This idea has been argued by Landa (1974) and to some extent by Scandura (1977). Ehrenpreis and Scandura (1974) found that it was possible to teach the higher level rules and algorithms as part of a mathematics course, and that students who received this training performed better on later tests than those who were taught in the traditional way. Thus, the cognitive approach holds some promise for changing the way that instruction is carried out.

Finally, the diagnosis and remediation of errors is a crucial problem in education. The BUGGY approach (Brown and Burton, 1978) encourages the hope that someday teachers will be able to give tests that indicate which bugs exist in a student's procedural knowledge rather than how many errors were made. It will then be easier to tailor remediation work to fit the needs of each child.

In recent years, cognitive psychologists have been able to generate process models for many different tasks in addition to basic computational arithmetic. The list of tasks for which process models have been described ranges from solving linear syllogisms (Potts, 1972) to judging whether a simple sentence matches a picture (Carpenter and Just, 1975). Process models thus offer a level of precision and depth that promises even greater progress in the future.

SUGGESTED READINGS

Brown, J. S., and R. R. Burton. Diagnostic models for procedural bugs in basic mathematical skills. *Cognitive Science*, 1978, *2*, 155–192. Descibes the BUGGY research projects discussed in this chapter.

Groen, G. J., and J. M. Parkman. A chronometric analysis of simple addition. *Psychological Review*, 1972, *79*, 329–343. Describes research on process models for simple one-digit addition.

Landa, L. N. *Algorithmization of learning and instruction.* Englewood Cliffs, N.J.: Educational Technology Publications, 1974. A summary of Russian research on teaching algorithms.

Miller, G. A., E. Galanter, and K. H. Pribram. *Plans and the structure of behavior.* New York: Holt, Rinehart & Winston, 1960. Classic book that argues for the use of process models as an alternative to S–R theories.

Resnick, L. B. Task analysis in instructional design: Some cases from mathematics. In D. Klahr (Ed.), *Cognition and instruction.* Hillsdale, N.J.: Erlbaum, 1976. Describes research on process models in simple one-digit subtraction.

4 Cognitive Structure Models

THE VERBAL KNOWLEDGE PROBLEM

Much of what we know about the world comes to us in the form of verbal information. For example, we are told that there was a major earthquake in San Francisco in 1906 or we read a story in the newspaper about a family that won the state lottery. When we listen to or read some verbal information we tend to remember some of it, forget some of it, and add to or change some of it. What is the process by which we acquire new verbal information and how do we store that knowledge in memory? These questions can be called the verbal knowledge problem.

For example, look at the passage given in Box 4.1. Read it over as you would normally read; then, put the passage aside and try to write a summary of the story. Now compare your summary to the actual text. Did you remember the main ideas? Did you forget some ideas? Did you add to or change some of the information?

This chapter will investigate new cognitive techniques for analyzing the structure of a person's verbal knowledge.

THE TRADITIONAL APPROACH

As Cofer (1976) has pointed out, there are two distinct traditional approaches to the verbal knowledge problem: the Ebbinghaus tradition and the Bartlett tradition. The Ebbinghaus tradition is based on the work of Ebbinghaus (1885), who was the first psychologist to study verbal learning and memory seriously. First, he made up lists of nonsense syllables with each syllable consisting of three letters. He then experimented on himself by memo-

There was once an old farmer who owned a very stubborn donkey. One evening the farmer was trying to put his donkey into its shed. First, the farmer pulled the donkey, but the donkey wouldn't move. Then the farmer pushed the donkey, but still the donkey wouldn't move. Finally, the farmer asked his dog to bark loudly at the donkey and thereby frighten him into the shed. But the dog refused. So then, the farmer asked his cat to scratch the dog so the dog would bark loudly and thereby frighten the donkey into the shed. But the cat replied, "I would gladly scratch the dog if only you would get me some milk." So the farmer went to his cow and asked for some milk to give to the cat. But the cow replied, "I would gladly give you some milk if only you would give me some hay." Thus, the farmer went to the haystack and got some hay. As soon as he gave the hay to the cow, the cow gave the farmer some milk. Then the farmer went to the cat and gave the milk to the cat. As soon as the cat got the milk, it began to scratch the dog. As soon as the cat scratched the dog, the dog began to bark loudly. The barking so frightened the donkey that it jumped immediately into its shed.

Source: Perry W. Thorndyke, "Cognitive Structures in Comprehension and Memory of Narrative Discourse," *Cognitive Psychology*, vol. 9, 1977, pp. 77–110.

Box 4.1 The Old Farmer and the Donkey

rizing and then recalling the lists under a number of different conditions. He found, for example, that he remembered more syllables if he practiced the list more and he remembered fewer syllables if he waited a long time for a test. While these may not seem like startling findings, they did form the basis for much subsequent work. As you may have guessed, Ebbinghaus' theoretical approach was a version of S–R associationism; the stimuli went into memory, the response came out, and the main thing to be measured was how much was remembered.

The Bartlett (1932) tradition stands in sharp contrast to the Ebbinghaus tradition. Bartlett was interested in the cognitive question of how verbal knowledge is organized in a person's head rather than the behavioral question of how much is remembered. Instead of using lists of nonsense syllables as his stimuli, Bartlett used an actual story. For example, he asked his subjects to read a folk story from an unfamiliar culture, repeat the story for the next person, let that person reproduce the story for the next person, and so on. By the time the story reached the last person in line, it had been completely changed. Many details and names were missing. References to spirits and ghosts were eliminated. New events were added so that the story would "make sense." In short, Bartlett concluded that humans do not passively record verbal information and randomly forget some of it. Rather humans make "an effort after meaning"—an active attempt to make sense out of the story or information, an attempt to fit the new story to what they already know and are familiar with.

Unfortunately, Bartlett was never able to be very precise about his concept of "effort after meaning," and his work remained largely ignored for decades. On the other hand, Ebbinghaus attracted many followers who worked in his tradition of using word lists. However, while his work was precise and experimentally well controlled, it did not really deal with the complex problems of memory for prose. The dilemma, then, was that the Bartlett tradition raised interesting ideas but lacked the needed tools for analysis, while the Ebbinghaus tradition provided the needed rigor and precision but failed to address the issue of complex verbal learning. However, with the rebirth of interest in cognitive psychology, the questions raised by Bartlett and the tradition of rigorous analysis established by Ebbinghaus have finally come together.

THE COGNITIVE APPROACH

The cognitive approach to the verbal knowledge problem involves an attempt to analyze verbal knowledge into parts and to indicate the structure into which these parts fit. Thus, a structure model of a person's verbal knowledge generally consists of elements and relations among them. Two of the most useful techniques for representing verbal knowledge are networks and trees. A network is a diagram that indicates each of the major elements by a box or oval, with lines among them that specify relations. A tree consists of a diagram that begins at the top and branches to a second level, and then branches from that level to a third, and so

on. Let's examine how these work by focusing on how to represent the knowledge in a sentence, and then in a simple narrative.

You are already familiar with sentence grammar—the rules for
breaking a sentence into its parts and relations. For example,
consider the sentence, *In the afternoon, I get very tired of
working.* It can be broken down into a qualifying phrase (*In the
afternoon*) and a major clause (*I get very tired of working*). These
parts can be broken down further. The major clause consists of a
subject (*I*) and a predicate (*get very tired of working*); the predicate consists of a verb phrase (*get very tired*) and an object (*of
working*); the verb phrase can be broken into a verb (*get tired*)
and an adverb (*very*); while the object decomposes into a preposition (*of*) and a noun (*working*).

Box 4.2 shows how this sentence can be represented as a tree.
The top of the tree is the entire sentence. Then, at the first level
from the top there is a break, based on the rule,

Sentence = Qualifying phrase + Major clause

At the next lower level, the two clauses are broken down using
the rules,

Qualifying phrase = Preposition + Noun phrase

Major clause = Subject + Predicate

At the next level we can apply the following rules for breaking
down the test:

Noun phrase = Noun + article

Predicate = Verb phrase + Object phrase

Finally, the last rules applied at the bottom of the tree are

Verb phrase = Verb + Adverb

Object phrase = Preposition + Noun

Thus, under the tree we can now see how each part of the sentence fits into the overall structure.

The rules for breaking a sentence down into its parts such as
those listed above are called parsing rules. You may not have been

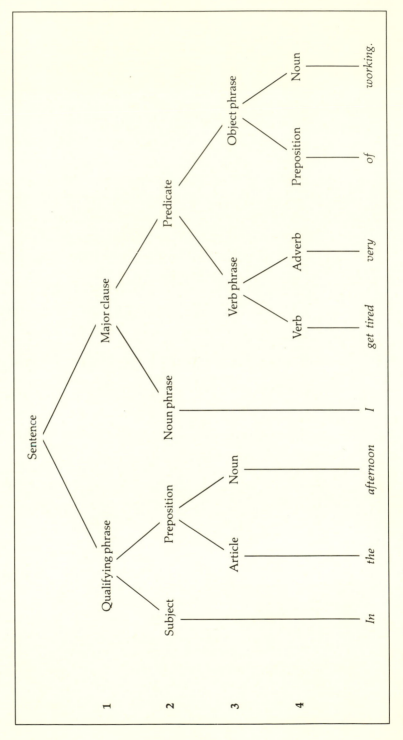

Box 4.2 Tree Structure for a Sentence

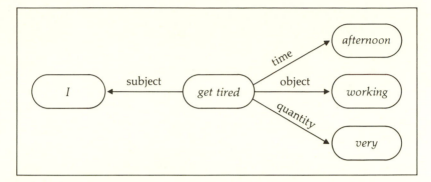

Box 4.3   Network Structure for a Sentence

taught exactly these rules or this type of terminology in your English courses. However, there is some evidence (Anderson and Bower, 1975; Kintsch, 1974) that people do use rules like these for comprehending sentences.

Box 4.3 shows another way of representing the sentence, a network graph. We take the main predicate, *get tired*, as the central node of the network. Then we find the arguments for this predicate, each of which holds a certain relationship to it. For example, we know that a predicate generally has a subject; that is, the person who *gets tired*. In this case the subject is *I*. Also, a predicate needs an object; *I get tired* of what? In this case, the object is *working.*The predicate may also need a setting such as time and place; that is, *get tired* when? In this case, the time argument is *in the afternoon*. The predicate may even have some arguments that modify it, such as *get tired* how much? In this case the argument *very* has a relation to the predicate. Thus, for any predicate in a sentence we have expectations concerning which types of arguments should go with it. In this case, we can summarize the arguments as follows:

> *Get tired*—subject: *I*, object: *working,*
> time: *afternoon*, quantity: *very*

This set of rules for finding the relationships between a predicate and its argument is called case grammar (Fillmore, 1968) because each type of relation is specified. The network shown in Box 4.3 specifies the predicate, the arguments, and each of the case relations.

The parsing rules or case grammar for sentences make it easier to represent the elements and overall structure of a sentence— that is, they provide a structure model for the information in a sentence. However, suppose we want to analyze a larger chunk of information, such as a simple narrative, into its parts and rela- tions. Think of stories that you know, like a children's fairy tale or the story in Box 4.1. What are the major parts of such stories and how do they fit together? In essence, you need to determine what cognitive psychologists have called the story grammar. Since we are already familiar with sentence grammar (such as shown in Boxes 4.2 and 4.3), can we apply the same type of analysis to entire stories? For example, we have suggested that people have certain expectations of a sentence: a predicate will have a subject and object, and so forth. Can we specify the same sort of expec- tations—like parsing rules or case grammar—for stories?

The basic units that make up a sentence are words. What are the larger units that make up a story? In general, let's say that the units are simple sentences or clauses that express one event or one state. Thus, the first thing we can do in analyzing a story is to break it down into a list of simple sentences with each sentence either expressing one event or describing one state.

Now that we have specified the building blocks for our story grammar—states and events—we need to describe the structure into which they can be fit. What are the rules that specify the relations among simple sentences? Thorndyke (1977), building on the work of Rumelhart (1975), has suggested some parsing rules. First, a story can generally be broken down into four parts: We expect a setting, a theme, a plot, and finally we expect that the plot will be resolved. This basic grammar can be summarized as follows:

Rule 1: Story = Setting + Theme + Plot + Resolution

Each of the simple sentences (that is, events and states) should fit into one of these four categories.

Now we can go on and analyze each of these components of a story. A setting generally consists of some characters, a location, and a time. We can summarize this as:

Rule 2: Setting = Characters + Location + Time

We will not break these down any further. In a story we will thus expect to find some event(s) and/or state(s) that refer to characters, some that refer to location, and some that refer to time.

Next comes the theme. A theme of a story generally consists of some goal; sometimes there is an event or series of events that lead up to the need for this goal. This can be summarized as:

Rule 3: Theme = Event(s) + Goal

A goal is just a state. An event, of course, is expressed in a simple sentence as an event.

Now comes the plot. The plot consists of a series of episodes, and can be summarized as:

Rule 4: Plot = Episode(s)

What is an episode? An episode consists of a subgoal, one or more attempts to reach the subgoal, and the outcome of the attempt(s). This can be summarized as:

Rule 4a: Episode = Subgoal + Attempt(s) + Outcome

A new episode can also have its own attempts, and so on.

This brings us at last to the resolution. The resolution consists of an event or a state.

Rule 5: Resolution = Event or State

These few basic rules form the basis of a story grammar that is involved in many types of narratives. They have been modified from a similar set of rules described by Rumelhart (1975) and by Thorndyke (1977), for a variety of stories.

This type of story grammar offers an advance over earlier work, because it allows us to state more precisely what might be meant by "effort after meaning." If adults carry around these story grammar rules and try to use them when they read a story, this means that they try to fit the incoming story into these pre-existing structures for a story. They expect a setting, theme, plot and resolution, and so on. Comprehension and storage of story information may depend on how well the presented information can fit into our story grammar structures.

EXAMPLES OF THE COGNITIVE APPROACH

Thorndyke (1977) has provided a good example of how the analysis of verbal knowledge can be carried out and tested. He asked college students to listen to or read a story such as "The Old Farmer and the Donkey" (given in Box 4.1). Some subjects were given the complete story in its normal order (story group), some were given the story in random order (random group).

One of the major problems in this study was to develop a way to represent the structure of the story—that is, a structure model for the verbal information. First, Thorndyke broke the passage down into propositions, with each proposition presenting either one simple event or one simple state. There turn out to be 35 simple events and states. These are listed in Box 4.4.

Next, it is necessary to arrange these propositions into a structure, as shown in Box 4.5. Using the parsing rules for stories described in the previous section, we can break a story into four parts: setting, theme, plot, and resolution.

Let's look first at the setting of "The Old Farmer and the Donkey." The setting can be broken down into characters, location, and time. The characters are the old farmer (stated in proposition 1) and the donkey (stated in proposition 2). Thus, propositions 1 and 2 fit into the "Characters" part of the tree diagram shown in Box 4.5. We might also suppose that the location is a farm, but since there is no proposition that states this, we will ignore it for now.

Since there are no other propositions that refer to setting, let's move on to the second major section, the theme. Remember that the theme consists of a major goal; this goal may have some event that leads up to it or, as in the present case, may not. What is the

1. There was once an old farmer
2. who owned a very stubborn donkey.
3. One evening the farmer was trying to put his donkey into its shed.
4. First, the farmer pulled the donkey,
5. but the donkey wouldn't move.
6. Then the farmer pushed the donkey,
7. but still the donkey wouldn't move.
8. Finally, the farmer asked his dog
9. to bark loudly at the donkey
10. and thereby frighten him into the shed.
11. But the dog refused.
12. So then, the farmer asked his cat
13. to scratch the dog
14. so the dog would bark loudly
15. and thereby frighten the donkey into the shed.
16. But the cat replied, "I would gladly scratch the dog
17. if only you would get me some milk."
18. So the farmer went to his cow
19. and asked for some milk
20. to give to the cat.
21. But the cow replied,
22. "I would gladly give you some milk
23. if only you would give me some hay."
24. Thus, the farmer went to the haystack
25. and got some hay.
26. As soon as he gave the hay to the cow,
27. the cow gave the farmer some milk.
28. Then the farmer went to the cat
29. and gave the milk to the cat.
30. As soon as the cat got the milk,
31. it began to scratch the dog.
32. As soon as the cat scratched the dog,
33. the dog began to bark loudly.
34. The barking so frightened the donkey
35. that it jumped immediately into its shed.

Source: Perry W. Thorndyke, "Cognitive Structures in Comprehension and Memory of Narrative Discourse," *Cognitive Psychology*, vol. 9, 1977, pp. 77–110.

Box 4.4   List of Events and States for
"The Old Farmer and the Donkey"

main goal discussed in this story? The farmer wants to get the donkey into its shed. Thus, the theme of the story is presented in proposition 3, which states the goal.

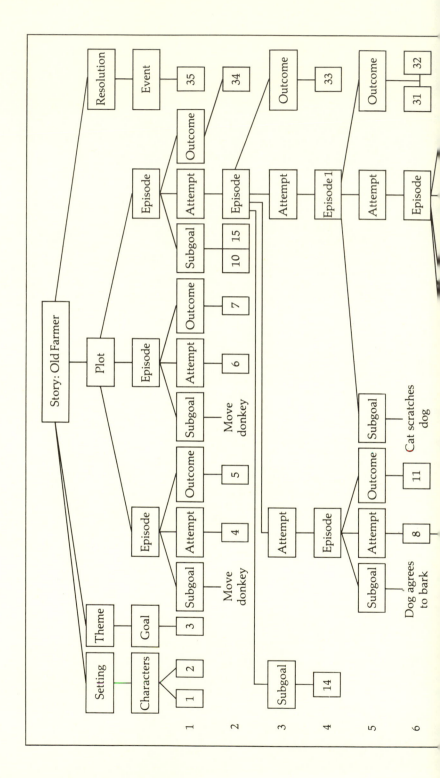

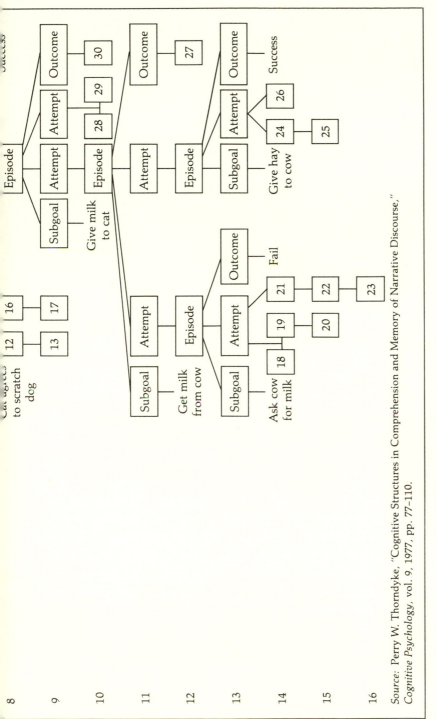

Source: Perry W. Thorndyke, "Cognitive Structures in Comprehension and Memory of Narrative Discourse," *Cognitive Psychology*, vol. 9, 1977, pp. 77–110.

Box 4.5 Tree Structure for "The Old Farmer and the Donkey"

Since there are no other propositions that deal with this goal or the events leading up to it, let's move on to the third section of the story, the plot. Remember that the plot is made up of many episodes, and that episodes consist of subgoals, attempts, and outcomes. In the first episode, the new subgoal is to pull the donkey; this is attempted (proposition 4) but fails (proposition 5). In the second episode, the subgoal of pushing the donkey is attempted (proposition 6) but also fails (proposition 7). In the next episode, there is a new subgoal—to frighten the donkey, as stated in propositions 10 and 15—and the eventual outcome is success, as stated in proposition 34. However, in the attempt to satisfy this subgoal, there are many new episodes with new subgoals like "have cat scratch dog," "make dog bark," "get milk from cow," and so on. These are listed under the plot in Box 4.5. Finally, the last element of a story that a person expects is a resolution. In "The Old Farmer and the Donkey" the story's main goal—getting the donkey in the shed—is achieved, so proposition 35 states the resolution. Thus, the "Old Farmer and the Donkey" story can be fit into the general structure laid out earlier: there is a clear setting (consisting of two characters), a theme (consisting of the goal of getting the donkey into the shed), a long, complicated plot that begins with the subgoals of pushing, pulling, and finally scaring the donkey and ends with the outcome of scaring the donkey, and a resolution (consisting of getting the donkey into the shed).

Rumelhart (1975) and Thorndyke (1977) have been able to create tree structures like these for a variety of stories. However, Thorndyke was also interested in testing to see whether the structure model he created was a useful or valid one. In order to test his story grammar he asked subjects to recall the story. He predicted that people would recall the propositions that fit high in the tree, since these are most central to the structure of the story. The highest propositions in the tree are 1, 2, 3, and 35—these give the characters, the theme, and the resolution. The next highest are 4, 5, 6, 7, 10, 15, and 34, which give the first simple subgoals and attempts and outcomes. The rest of the propositions are lower because they involve episodes of the subgoal of scaring the donkey.

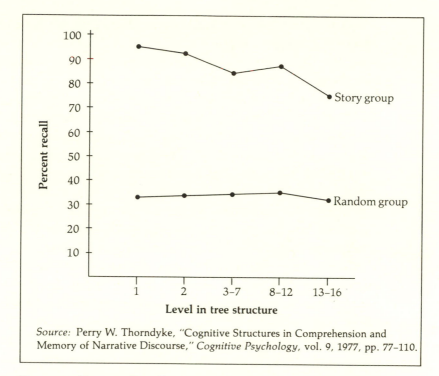

Source: Perry W. Thorndyke, "Cognitive Structures in Comprehension and Memory of Narrative Discourse," *Cognitive Psychology*, vol. 9, 1977, pp. 77–110.

Box 4.6 Percent Recall of "The Old Farmer and the Donkey" Story by Level in the Tree Structure

Box 4.6 shows the percentage of propositions recalled, by level in the hierarchy, for the two groups. The story group recalled almost all of the level 1 information, but less and less of the information in successively lower levels of the tree. The random group, however, shows an entirely different pattern. Since they apparently did not treat the information as forming an organized story, they recalled equivalent amounts from each level of the hierarchy. Thus, the story group behaved as if each reader had tried to build a tree like the one given in the figure and worked from the top down; the random group, however, was not able to build such a structure and remembered the information in a much less organized way.

As another test, Thorndyke produced some versions of the story that did not contain the theme or did not state it until the end. If readers cannot determine the theme, it will be very difficult for them to build a useful internal tree for a story. Thus, he predicted that recall of the remaining propositions would be poorer for these subjects than for subjects who had the theme stated early in the story (that is, the normal story). As predicted, removing or postponing the theme had a strong negative effect on recall, although it was not as harmful as placing the propositions in random order.

Finally, Thorndyke conducted another test of his analysis of cognitive structure for the stories he used. Suppose that people comprehend stories by trying to fit the propositions into a story grammar structure. If two stories are read in order, and if the second has the same structure as the first, but different content, then it should be easier to understand since the reader has just built that particular structure. Understanding the second story means simply fitting the new characters and events into a familiar structure. However, if a new structure is used in the second story, it should be harder to understand because the reader must break out of his previous way of structuring the story and build a new tree. When Thorndyke tested this idea he again found supporting evidence for his predictions. Repeating the same structure across two different stories helped recall, but repeating the same content (characters and events) in a new structure caused interference in recall.

In summary, Thorndyke was successful in analyzing a passage into its parts, determining the structure into which the parts might fit, and testing to see whether humans actually tend to build this structure when they comprehend stories. As you can see, a system like Thorndyke's deals with learning and memory for real-world, meaningful verbal information; thus this line of research is an advance over Ebbinghaus' work on lists of nonsense syllables. The cognitive structures required to represent meaningful verbal information are quite different from those involved in rote learning situations such as Ebbinghaus used. This line of research is also an advance over Bartlett's work on memory for stories. Thorndyke's analysis is far more detailed and precise than Bartlett's and allows for more specific predictions.

APPLYING WHAT YOU'VE LEARNED

In the previous section, we showed how the story grammar approach can be used to specify the structure that a person is likely to acquire from a narrative when he is making "an effort after meaning." The story grammar described in the previous section was developed for use in a wide variety of stories. It is a general purpose story grammar. However, suppose you wanted to develop a more specific set of rules for a more restricted set of stories.

For example, suppose that I said I wanted to tell you about what happened to me when I went and ate at Joe's restaurant last night. You probably have a certain set of expectations when you read or listen to an episode about someone going into a restaurant. Based on your general experience with restaurants, you have some idea of the script for a restaurant episode; as you read or listen to the story you try to fill in the general script with the specific events and situations in the particular story.

Take a minute to write down the main scenes you would expect in a restaurant script; for each scene write down the general events you would expect.

If you are having trouble, first try to list the cast of characters, such as customer, host/hostess, waiter/waitress, chef, cashier, and others. Now, what are the major scenes? The first scene, for example, might be entering and getting seated. What are all of the events you would expect to take place in this scene?

Box 4.7 gives a summary of the restaurant script suggested by Schank and Abelson (1977) in their book, *Scripts, Plans, Goals, and Understanding*. These authors argue that, in addition to general story grammars, adults also have specialized scripts for recurring episodes in their experience. Their version of the res-

---

Schema: Restaurant.

Characters: Customer, hostess, waiter, chef, cashier.

Scene 1: Entering.
        Customer goes into restaurant.
        Customer finds a place to sit.
          He may find it himself
          He may be seated by a hostess.
            He asks the hostess for a table.
            She gives him permission to go to the table.
        Customer goes and sits at the table.

Scene 2: Ordering.
        Customer receives a menu.
        Customer reads it.
        Customer decides what to order.
        Waiter takes the order.
          Waiter sees the customer.
          Waiter goes to the customer.
          Customer orders what he wants.
        Chef cooks the meal.

Scene 3: Eating.
        After some time the waiter brings the meal from the chef.
        Customer eats the meal.

Scene 4: Exiting.
        Customer asks the waiter for the check.
        Waiter gives the check to the customer.
        Customer leaves a tip.
          The size of the tip depends on the goodness of the service.
        Customer pays the cashier.
        Customer leaves the restaurant.

Source: D. E. Rumelhart, *Introduction to Human Information Processing.* New York: Wiley, 1977.

Box 4.7   Schank and Abelson's Restaurant Script

taurant script consists of four scenes: entering, ordering, eating, and exiting. How does yours compare?

    Schank and Abelson also argue that people use scripts for comprehending verbal information. For example, when someone tells you something in a conversation, you try to find the appropriate script in your memory; you ask yourself, "Is this information from a restaurant script, or a taking-the-plane script, or a going-to-in-laws script?" and so on. Once you figure out which script is appropriate, it is much easier to comprehend what is being said.

Suppose you are at a party, and a friend tells you the following story.

> Sally and John and Beth and I decided to go out for dinner last night. Well, we found a table right away and sat down. I got up and ordered the specialty of the house for everybody. It didn't take long for the meals to be ready. I paid for the food, and brought it back to the table. Everyone ate and said the meal was delicious. Then we cleaned up and left.

When you hear this episode, you might be tempted to use your standard restaurant script (as shown in Box 4.7) to understand it. However, as you try to fit the events in the episode into the script, you might have some problems. Suppose you use the Schank and Abelson script. Which events would fit into the script and which events would not? Also, where would they fit into the script?

The episode can be broken down into the following events:

1. Sally and John and Beth and I decided to go out for dinner last night.
2. We found a table right away and sat down.
3. I got up,
4. and ordered the specialty of the house for everyone.
5. It didn't take long for the meals to be ready.
6. I paid for the food,
7. and brought it back to the table.
8. Everyone ate
9. and said the meal was delicious.
10. Then we cleaned up
11. and left.

As you try to fit these events into the restaurant script you would probably find the following:

1. A signal to you to use the restaurant script.
2. Fits into the entering scene.

3. Seems to belong in the ordering scene but does not fit the script since one does not normally get up to order. This might cause you to change your script or to just try to fit event 3 in any way. One way to fit it in is to ignore it. Another is to assume that it is a formal restaurant and it is polite to stand up when ordering.

4. Seems to fit the ordering scene.

5. Fits the eating scene.

6. Does not fit. It is out of order. Again, you could change your script at this point or try to fit in this event in some other way.

7. Also does not fit. The waiter or waitress is supposed to bring the food, according to the script. You should become very skeptical at this point concerning your script. It just does not seem to be able to hold the events in the story.

8, 9. Fit the eating scene.

10. Seems related to the exiting scene but does not fit any of the expected events in the script. By now you should see clearly that a different script is needed.

11. Fits the exiting scene.

As you can see, most of the events fit the script, but there are many that don't. As you listen to the story you might decide that you need to use a modified script—the McDonald's restaurant script, for example. If you use this script, the events in the story fit the expected structure much better: one gets up to order and carry back the food, cleans up before leaving, pays before eating, and so on.

As you can see, one important source of misunderstanding or failure to communicate may be that the sender and receiver are using different scripts. It is useful to tell the listener early in the conversation which script he or she should be using for organizing the statements that will follow. The concept of a script is similar to other concepts such as Minsky's (1975) "frame" or Bransford's (1979) "schema."

FURTHER APPLICATIONS OF STRUCTURE MODELS

The work on story grammars (broadly defined) is a very new area in cognitive psychology, and yet it has already demonstrated much success. Apparently, it is possible to describe the cognitive structures that people acquire from stories and the rules they use for understanding and building them. Results similar to those described in this chapter have also been reported by Kintsch and his colleagues (Kintsch, 1974, 1976; Kintsch and van Dijk, 1978) and by Meyer (1975).

If people have a set of grammar rules about narratives, it is likely that they also have other grammar systems for use in understanding other types of verbal information. For example, Kintsch (1974) has suggested a macrostructure for scientific reports, and Spilich, Vesonder, Chiesi, and Voss (1979) have developed a macrostructure for understanding the radio broadcast of a baseball game. Although the particular rules are different, it is possible to represent a scientific report or a baseball game transcript as a tree diagram and to predict that the upper levels of the tree will be better remembered. As work progresses, there will likely be an explosion of grammars for many particular types of verbal information in addition to stories.

If cognitive psychologists are able to specify the grammars for particular types of information, it seems likely that we can do a better job of presenting information. For example, Stein and Nezworski (1978) found that when stories are presented in the optimal order as prescribed by a story grammar, people remember much more of the story than when the story is slightly or greatly at variance with the expected order. Also, Thorndyke (1977) found that practice with a particular story structure aided comprehension of a story with the same structure. The work on story grammars may eventually lead to prescriptions for writers on how to make sure their prose meshes with people's expected grammars.

An understanding of the structure of verbal knowledge holds other promises as well. If someone is having trouble reading and comprehending a textbook in a certain area, such as American history, perhaps the appropriate remediation would be to make the grammar of the history book more explicit. By giving the student a grammar system for organizing the prose, one could be more confident that the important topics would be remembered and organized well. Thus, it seems likely that we may someday teach people about the grammars of subject areas (like stories) in the same sort of way we now teach students about the grammar of sentences. Recently, Kintsch and van Dijk (1978) have suggested a precise model of how humans read, based on the idea that we try to build hierarchical structures for the information. As we test and refine such theories, we may be in a much better position to teach people how to read in specific disciplines.

Finally, the story grammar approach provides a new way of measuring what a given person knows about a given topic. Instead of saying that "Sharon got 85 percent correct on a test covering the chapter on electricity," we can specify how Sharon has organized the information. We can pinpoint areas that are missing; perhaps part of the grammar is not being used, such as remembering the causal link between two events. New techniques for measuring and representing cognitive structure could lead to better evaluation, diagnosis, and remediation.

In summary, cognitive psychologists have developed systems for describing the verbal knowledge that one acquires from prose. Even the stories that Bartlett used 50 years ago have finally been subjected to story grammar analysis (Mandler and Johnson, 1977). Yet much remains to be done; this frontier, which did not exist a decade ago, is far from being well mapped.

SUGGESTED READINGS

Kintsch, W. Memory for prose. In C. N. Cofer (Ed.),
   The structure of memory. San Francisco: W. H. Freeman and
   Company, 1976. Describes a research project concerned with
   the representation of verbal knowledge in memory.

Meyer, B. J. F. *The organization of prose and its effects on
   memory.* Amsterdam: North-Holland, 1975. Describes a
   system for analyzing passages using a case grammar
   approach.

Rumelhart, D. E. Notes on a schema for stories. In D. G.
   Bobrow and A. M. Collins (Eds.), *Representation and
   understanding: Studies in cognitive science.* New York:

Academic Press, 1975. Describes a system for analyzing stories into tree structures such as those described in this chapter.

Schank, R. C., and R. P. Abelson. *Scripts, plans, goals, and understanding.* Hillsdale, N.J.: Erlbaum, 1977. Describes a system for representing knowledge about a story; makes heavy use of computer terminology.

Thorndyke, P. W. Cognitive structures in comprehension and memory of narrative discourse. *Cognitive Psychology,* 1977, *9,* 77–110. Describes experiments on story grammars that are discussed in this chapter.

5 Cognitive Strategy Models

THE STRATEGY PROBLEM

When a person is confronted with a problem, there are many things he or she can bring to bear on it. So far we have examined three major features of the human cognitive system: the architecture of the information processing system (Chapter 2), the procedural knowledge brought to a task (Chapter 3), and the verbal knowledge brought to a task (Chapter 4). In this chapter, we will explore a fourth feature of the cognitive system—the general strategy for making the most efficient use of the memory stores, procedures, and knowledge structures that are available.

For example, suppose you had just learned the equations shown below:

$$work = weight \times distance \tag{1}$$

$$potential\ energy = weight \times height \tag{2}$$

$$power = \frac{work}{volume} \tag{3}$$

Now, if you had values for *weight*, *distance*, and *power*, could you determine the value for *volume*? As you attempt to solve this problem, talk aloud so that you are aware of the plan you follow.

In solving this problem, you must make use of your working memory as discussed in Chapter 2, so individual differences in the efficiency of operation of that memory store should affect problem-solving performance. You must also make use of the cognitive procedures discussed in Chapter 3, such as knowing how to multiply, divide, and use algebraic operations. In addition, you must form a knowledge structure as discussed in Chapter 4, in order to represent the three equations. However, as well as all of these factors, you must decide on some plan of attack, some general strategy for solving the problem.

One general strategy you could use is called working forward: Start with the givens (*weight, distance,* and *power*) and work towards the goal (*volume*). You notice that with *weight* and *distance* you can find *work* (using the first equation). With *work* and *power* you can find *volume* (third equation), which is the value you were asked about.

Another strategy is called working backwards, which involves starting with the goal (*volume*) and working towards the givens (*weight, distance,* and *power*). For example, to find *volume* you notice that you must know the values of *power* and *work* (in equation 3). You check your givens and see that you already know *power,* so all you need to find is *work*. To find *work,* you need to know the values of *weight* and *distance* (in equation 1). As you check your givens you notice that you have *weight* and *distance,* so you have solved the problem. (See Mayer and Greeno, 1975, for a more detailed description of strategies for solving this problem.)

These examples show that a person generally has several alternative strategies available in complex problem-solving tasks. The task of the cognitive psychologist is to specify clearly what these strategies (also called heuristics) are and how they are used. This can be called the strategy problem. The remainder of this chapter demonstrates how cognitive psychologists have attacked it.

THE TRADITIONAL APPROACH

Most of the early work on the strategy problem was based on informal observation of people—sometimes famous thinkers—in the act of solving some problem. One of the most common observations was that people tended to go through a series of stages in order to reach a solution. Although there was never much agreement on what the stages were, a typical set of stages was proclaimed by Wallas (1926) in his classic book, *The Art of Thought.*

The four stages in Wallas' system were: preparation (gathering information), incubation (putting the problem aside), illumination (a flash of insight), and verification (working through the solution). Polya (1957, 1968) also suggested a similar set of stages involved in mathematical problem solving.

Other early researchers, mainly gestalt psychologists, noticed that people set up subgoals in solving problems. For example, Duncker (1945) gave a subject the following problem: "Given a human being with an inoperable stomach tumor, and rays which destroy organic tissue at sufficient intensity, by what procedure can one free him of the tumor by these rays and at the same time avoid destroying the healthy tissue which surrounds it?" Duncker found that his subject hit upon a general solution to the problem —a general goal that drives the problem-solving process—before trying specific solutions. For example, a general goal would be "desensitize the healthy tissue" and a specific solution after that would be "immunize by adaptation to weak rays"; another general goal, "lower the intensity of the rays in the healthy tissue," suggests the specific solution "use a lens" (the correct solution). The entire set of goals and specific attempts is given in Box 5.1. Duncker's main point was that people tend to break a problem down into subgoals and then try to solve the subgoals.

Polya (1957, 1968) observed how students solve mathematics problems in high school courses. Like Duncker, he noticed that when a problem seems too difficult to solve, a good strategy is to break it down into smaller problems that can be solved. For example, if your job is to find the volume of a frustum (lower portion) of a pyramid, you may make up an easier subgoal—finding the volume of the entire pyramid. Thus, the idea of stages in problem solving and in particular the idea of subgoals were early contributions to the strategy problem. The general strategy people used seemed to involve breaking a problem down into its parts.

Unfortunately, these ideas never really got off the ground. They were stated so imprecisely that they seemed right but could not really be tested. No predictions could be made about human performance, and people's strategies could not be clearly described.

General Subgoal	Specific Subgoal	Specific Solution
	1a. Use free path to stomach.	1a. Esophagus
1. Avoid contact between rays and healthy tissue.	1b. Remove healthy tissue.	1b. Insert cannula.
	1c. Insert protecting wall.	1c. Feed substance which protects wall.
	1d. Displace tumor toward surface.	1d. By pressure.
2. Desensitize healthy tissue.	2a. Inject desensitizing chemical.	
	2b. Immunize by adaptation to weak rays.	
3. Lower intensity of rays through healthy tissue.	3a. Turn up intensity as ray hits tissue.	
	3b. Concentrate ray at place of tumor.	3b. Use lens.

Source: Adapted from K. Duncker, "On Problem Solving," *Psychological Monographs*, vol. 58, no. 270, 1945.

Box 5.1 Some Subgoals and Attempts in Solving Duncker's Tumor Problem

The required analytic tools were not yet available, and the concept of using subgoals remained a vague idea until the cognitive revolution. Many attempts—such as Polya's (1957) *How to Solve It*—were made to teach problem strategies, and with some success. Thus Polya and others raised interesting issues and challenged modern cognitive psychologists to get to work.

THE COGNITIVE APPROACH

It all began with computers. Electronic computers that could solve a variety of problems were developed during the late 1940s and early 1950s. As computer technology increased in sophistication, it became possible to program them to solve more and more complex problems. However, when computers were programmed to solve problems they needed several things: a set of memory stores and transformation processes (analogous to but quite different in structure from the human IPS discussed in Chapter 2), a set of procedures for accomplishing goals (as discussed in Chapter 3), a set of verbal knowledge (as discussed in Chapter 4), and a set of general strategies or heuristics for controlling the problem-solving process (as discussed in this chapter). Thus it became apparent that problem solving, at least in computers, required precise descriptions of problem-solving heuristics (or strategies). The same tools used for spelling out the strategies used in computers could be used, it seemed, to describe the strategies used by humans.

One of the earliest and best known computer programs related to this problem was called General Problem Solver (GPS). GPS was endowed by its creators (Ernst and Newell, 1969) with a powerful, general strategy that was supposed to enable it to solve a wide variety of problems. Ernst and Newell and, later, Newell and Simon (1972) asked humans to solve problems and to talk aloud as they worked, then abstracted from their subjects' reports the general strategy that they seemed to be using. Finally, the researchers tried to specify this strategy in precise detail so that they could program the problem-solving approach into GPS.

Ernst and Newell's book *GPS: A Case Study in Generality and Problem Solving* (1969) was a significant breakthrough. Until the invention of GPS, individual computer programs had been designed to specialize in just one type of problem; however, GPS was intended to possess a general problem-solving strategy that could be used in many different tasks. In all, Ernst and Newell tried GPS on 11 very different problems. These are listed in Box 5.2. Although GPS was able to solve these 11 problems, it did not always produce a goal structure that was similar to the way humans performed.

In 1972 Newell and Simon produced their monumental treatise, *Human Problem Solving*, which further developed the ideas presented in the earlier book. In addition, this book provided in-depth analysis of the strategies used by people solving cryptarith-

Missionaries and Cannibals

Three missionaries and three cannibals are on one side of a river and want to get to the other side. The only means of conveyance is a small boat with a capacity of two people. If at any time there are more cannibals than missionaries on either side of the river, those missionaries will be eaten by the cannibals. How can you get all six people across the river without any casualties?

Integration

Solve integration problems such as

$$\int [\sin^2(ct)\cos(ct) + t^{-1}]dt$$

Tower of Hanoi

There are three pegs and three (or more) disks. The disks vary in size and are placed on the first peg with the smallest on top and the largest on bottom. The problem is to move the disks to the third peg. The pegs must be moved one at a time, and a larger disk may never be placed on top of a smaller disk.

Proving Theorems

A famous theorem from predicate calculus is given.

Father and Sons

A father and his sons want to cross a river. They use a boat that has a maximum capacity of 200 pounds. Each son weighs 100 pounds and the father weighs 200 pounds. Assuming that the father and either son can operate the boat how can they get across the river?

Monkey Task

A monkey is in a room with a box and some bananas above him out of reach. How can the monkey get the bananas?

Three Coins

Three coins are on a table. The first and third show tails, while the second shows heads. A move consists of turning any two coins over. How can you use exactly three moves to get the coins to show all heads or all tails?

Parsing Sentences

Identify parts of speech in a sentence such as the following:

Free variables cause confusion.

Water Jug

Given a 5-gallon jug and 8-gallon jug, how can you get exactly 2 gallons of water?

Box 5.2 Eleven Problems for GPS (continued on next page)

Letter Series Completion

What is the next letter in the series:

B   C   B   D   B   E   ____

Bridges of Konigsberg

Given a city with seven bridges, can you start at one point and return to it after going over each bridge only one time?

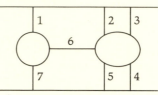

Source: Adapted from G. W. Ernst and A. Newell, *GPS: A Case Study in Generality and Problem Solving.* New York: Academic, 1969.

Answers:
Parsing Sentences: Free—adjective; variables—noun; cause—verb; confusion—object.
Water Jug: $5 + 5 - 8 = 2$ (Fill 5 and pour into 8, fill 5 and pour into 8, remainder is 2).
Letter Series: B.
Bridges: Impossible.

Box 5.2   Eleven Problems for GPS

metic problems, logic problems, and chess problems. The techniques for representing and testing models of human problem solving were clearly presented and are the basis for the discussion in this chapter.

How do you go about representing someone's problem-solving strategy? In order to understand how GPS does this, let's look at two separate ideas. First, a problem must be represented as a problem space. A problem space consists of the given state of the problem, the goal state of the problem, all possible operations that may be applied to any state to change it into another state, and all intermediate states of the problem. Box 5.3 shows an

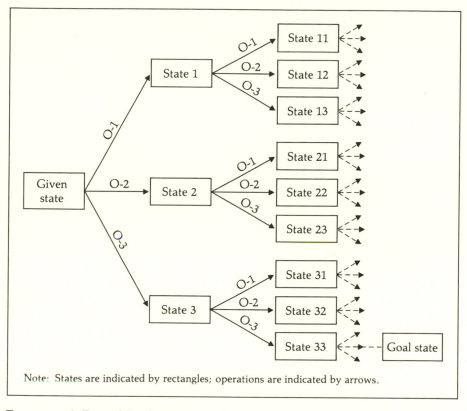

Note: States are indicated by rectangles; operations are indicated by arrows.

Box 5.3   A Partial Problem Space

example of a problem space with three possible operations. As you can see, there may be many useless paths (blind alleys) through the problem space.

Second, the solution to a problem involves a goal-directed searching through the problem space. In this case, problem solving involves finding the correct path from the given state, through some of the intermediate states, to the goal state. The important point here is that the search process is goal-directed. In general, people do not wander blindly or randomly around in the problem space. They have plans and subgoals. The particular planning strategy can be precisely represented in the GPS system.

The basic strategy for searching through the problem space in GPS is called means–ends analysis. Means–ends analysis is just one possible strategy that a person (or computer program) can use, but it is a general and powerful one. Means–ends analysis begins with a clearly specified problem space—all the allowable problem states and operators are specified. Then, the problem solver generates goals and attempts to find operators that can satisfy each goal; if a particular goal cannot be satisfied, a subgoal is created; only one subgoal is worked on at a time.

In GPS there are three general subgoals that can be used in means–ends analysis. They may be used repeatedly in a problem, but at any given point in problem solving only one can be used at a time. The three subgoals are

1. *Transform state A into state B.* This means that the problem is currently in one state (*A*) but you want it to be in some other state (*B*). In order to carry out this subgoal, you must compare state *A* to state *B*. If they are the same, you have succeeded and may go on. If they are different you must clearly specify what that difference (*D*) is. Once you have specified a difference *D* between states *A* and *B* you are ready to use a second subgoal (see below).

2. *Reduce difference D between state A and state B.* This means that you have located the difference *D* between *A* and *B*, and you would like to make the difference less. In order to carry out this subgoal, you must find some operator *Q* that is appropriate for the particular difference you have, and you must make sure that the operator *Q* can feasibly be applied to state *A*. Once you have found a relevant and feasible operator *Q*, you are ready to use a third subgoal (see below).

3. *Apply operator Q to state A.* This means that the problem is currently in state *A*, and that you would like to apply operator *Q* to state *A*. In order to carry out this subgoal, you compare the operator *Q* to the state *A*. If they match, you can apply the operator and produce a new state *A'*. If not, then you find the difference between the operator *Q* and the state *A'* and use subgoal 2 above to reduce it.

The three subgoals are summarized in Box 5.4. As you can see, each subgoal may also involve some of the other subgoals. One

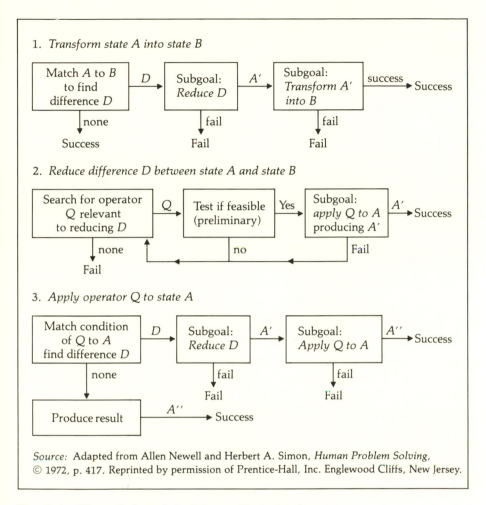

1. *Transform state A into state B*

2. *Reduce difference D between state A and state B*

3. *Apply operator Q to state A*

Source: Adapted from Allen Newell and Herbert A. Simon, *Human Problem Solving*, © 1972, p. 417. Reprinted by permission of Prentice-Hall, Inc. Englewood Cliffs, New Jersey.

Box 5.4 Three Subgoals in Means–Ends Analysis

way of thinking about the subgoals is that each has an input and an output. The *Transform A into B* subgoal starts with states *A* and *B* and outputs the difference *D* between them. The *Reduce D* subgoal starts with the difference *D* and outputs an operator *Q* that may be applicable to reducing the difference. The *Apply Q* subgoal takes state *A* and operator *Q* as the starting point and ends with a new state *A′* that is the result of applying *Q* to *A*.

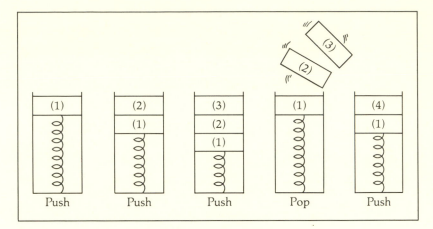

Box 5.5   Push-Down Pop-Up Goal Stack

In problem solving, a person begins with the goal of trans-
forming the given state into the goal state. As you can see, this is a
Transform A into B subgoal. Let's make this the top goal in a
push-down pop-up stack as shown in Box 5.5. We put in the top
goal (1) and find that there is a difference *D*. Thus, the following
subgoal might be *Reduce the difference D.* We have not yet solved
the top goal so it stays in the stack, but we put subgoal (2) on top
of it. In order to accomplish subgoal (2) we must find an operator
and apply it. Let's say we find an operator *Q* and proceed to the
next subgoal (3): *Apply operator Q to state A.* Thus, we now put
subgoal (3) on top of our stack. We try to accomplish this subgoal
and are able to apply *Q* directly to state *A.* Thus subgoal (3) is
complete and can be popped off. This also satisfies subgoal (2), so
it pops off, and now we return to goal (1). We can say that goal (1)
is reinstated, and we must check to see if state *A* is different from
state *B.* If so, we push on a new subgoal (4) of reducing the difference, and so on. As you can see, the push-down pop-up stack
allows you to work on only one subgoal at a time and makes you
set up a new subgoal if you cannot solve the current one. Thus,
the three general subgoals and the stack provide a precise
mechanism for representing the strategy of the problem solver.

So far, we have examined two major representational tools that can be used in solving the strategy problem. These tools are a technique for specifying the problem space and a technique for specifying the goal structure of a problem. In the next section of this chapter we will show how these techiques can be applied to a real-world problem-solving situation—solving algebra problems.

EXAMPLES OF THE COGNITIVE APPROACH

Consider the problem of solving for x in the following equation:

$$2(3x - 11) = 3x + 8.$$

Assuming that the problem solver uses means–ends analysis, how can we represent the problem-solving process?

First, we need to construct a problem space. The initial state is

$$2(3x - 11) = 3x + 8$$

and the goal state is

$$x = \text{some number}$$

The allowable operators involve addition, subtraction, multiplication, and division of numbers and variables as specified by the rules of algebra. For purposes of this discussion let's define five operators:

Move number. Performing the same arithmetic operation on a number on both sides of the equation, such as subtracting 8 from both sides.

Move variable. Performing the same arithmetic operation on a variable on both sides of the equation, such as subtracting $3x$ from both sides.

Combine numbers. Performing an indicated arithmetic operation on two numbers on one side of the equation, such as changing $22 + 8$ into 30.

Combine variables. Performing an indicated arithmetic operation on two variables on the same side of the equation, such as changing $6x - 3x$ into $3x$.

Compute parens. Performing an indicated arithmetic operation between parentheses involving numbers and variables, such as changing $2(3x - 11)$ into $6x - 22$.

Name	Condition	Action
Move variable (MV)	x variable is on right side of equation.	Perform corresponding arithmetic operations to both sides, so as to move the x variable from right to left.
Move number (MN)	Number is on left side of equation.	Perform corresponding arithmetic operations to both sides, so as to move the number from left to right.
Combine variables (CV)	Two x variables on one side of equation.	Perform indicated operation so as to combine them into one x variable.
Combine numbers (CN)	Two numbers on one side of equation.	Perform indicated operation so as to combine them into one number.
Compute parentheses (CP)	Operation is to be distributed across parentheses.	Perform indicated operations so as to eliminate the parentheses.

Box 5.6   Condition–Action Chart

The conditions and actions implied by these five operators are summarized in Box 5.6.

To generate the intermediate states for the problem space, let's start with the given state and see what operators can be applied. We can apply *Move number* to the given state in order to get

$$2(3x - 11) - 8 = 3x$$

We can apply *Move variable* to the given state in order to get

$$2(3x - 11) - 3x = 8$$

We cannot apply *Combine numbers* or *Combine variables* to the given state because there are not two numbers or two variables on one side. We can apply *Compute parens* to the given state on the left side to get

$$6x - 22 = 3x + 8$$

Thus from the initial state there are three states in the first level of the problem space.

Where can we go from each of these states? If we are in the state

$$2(3x - 11) - 8 = 3x$$

we can move back to the start by *Move number,* or we can use *Move variable* to get

$$2(3x - 11) - 8 - 3x = 0$$

or we can apply *Compute parens* to get

$$6x - 22 - 8 = 3x$$

If we are in the state

$$2(3x - 11) - 3x = 8$$

we can get back to the given state by applying *Move variable* or we can apply *Move number* to get

$$2(3x - 11) - 8 - 3x = 0$$

or we can apply *Compute parens* to get

$$6x - 22 - 3x = 8$$

If we are in the state

$$6x - 22 = 3x + 8$$

we can use *Move variable* to get

$$6x - 22 - 3x = 8$$

or we can use *Move number* to get

$$6x = 3x + 8 + 22$$

These equations form the second level in the problem space. Part of the problem space is indicated in Box 5.7. Notice that one of the

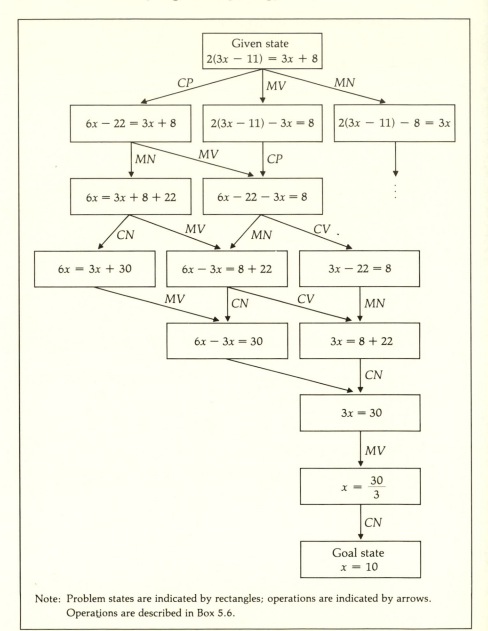

Box 5.7 Part of the Problem Space for $2(3x - 11) = 3x + 8$

five operators is applied in moving from each state to the next.

The next task is to represent the search process that someone goes through in moving across the problem space. We need to bring out our three subgoals as described in the previous section —*Transform A into B, Reduce D,* and *Apply Q*—and we need to bring out our push-down pop-up stack. These are general tools for representing the search process, but we also need to make some specific prescriptions concerning which operator (*Q*) should be applied under which conditions. There are five operators in the problem, and the goal state has *x* on the left side and a number on the right side of the equation. When there is an individual number on the left side of the equation, then we can apply the *Move number* operator. When there is an individual variable on the right side of the equation, then we can apply the *Move variable* operator. When there are two numbers on one side of the equation with an indicated arithmetic operation, we can apply the *Combine numbers* operator. When there are two variables on one side of the equation with an indicated arithmetic operation, we can apply the *Combine variables* operator. When there is an arithmetic operation indicated by parentheses, we can apply the *Compute parens* operator. (See Box 5.6.)

Now we are ready to start the show. You can use Box 5.8 to follow the problem-solving process. Our goal is to transform the given state into the goal state, so that is the top goal in the push-down pop-up stack. When we check for differences we find that there is a single variable on the right, a single number on the left, and a parentheses operation on the left. Since goal (1) cannot be achieved immediately, we create subgoal (2) and put it on top of the stack. This subgoal is to reduce the difference (that is, eliminate the problem that there is a variable on the right). Looking at the condition–action chart in Box 5.6, we see that the appropriate operation is *Move variable*. Thus, we create subgoal (3) to apply this operator; it works, and we create a new problem state. Subgoals (2) and (3) have been popped off, and we return to the original goal. However, there is still a difference between the present state of the problem and the goal state: There is a number on the left side, two separate variables are apart on the left side,

Subgoals in Stack*	Type of Subgoal	Statement of Subgoal	Success
(1)	*Transform*	Find value for x.	No: x on right, number on left, parens.
(2)(1)	*Reduce*	Get x to left.	Yes: Use *MV*.
(3)(2)(1)	*Apply*	Apply *MV*.	Yes: $2(3x-11)-3x=8$.
(1)	*Transform*	Find value for x.	No: Number on left, 2 x's apart, parens.
(4)(1)	*Reduce*	Get x's together.	Yes: Use *CV*.
(5)(4)(1)	*Apply*	Apply *CV*.	No: Parens.
(6)(5)(4)(1)	*Reduce*	Eliminate parentheses.	Yes: Use *CP*.
(7)(6)(5)(4)(1)	*Apply*	Apply *CP*.	Yes: $6x-22-3x=8$.
(5)(4)(1)	*Apply*	Apply *CV*.	Yes: $3x-22=8$.
(1)	*Transform*	Find value for x.	No: Number on left.
(8)(1)	*Reduce*	Get number to right.	Yes: Use *MN*.
(9)(8)(1)	*Apply*	Apply *MN*.	Yes: $3x=8+22$.
(1)	*Transform*	Find value for x.	No: 2 numbers apart, number on left.
(10)(1)	*Reduce*	Get numbers together.	Yes: Use *CN*.
(11)(10)(1)	*Apply*	Apply *CN*.	Yes: $3x=30$.
(1)	*Transform*	Find value for x.	No: Number on left.
(12)(1)	*Reduce*	Get number to right.	Yes: Use *MN*.
(13)(12)(1)	*Apply*	Apply *MN*.	Yes: $x=\frac{30}{3}$
(1)	*Transform*	Find value for x.	No: 2 numbers apart.
(14)(1)	*Reduce*	Get numbers together.	Yes: Use *CN*.
(15)(14)(1)	*Apply*	Apply *CN*.	Yes: $x=10$.
(1)	*Transform*	Find value for x.	Yes: $x=10$.

*Note: The push-down pop-up stack includes the overall goal [goal (1)] as well as subgoals.

Box 5.8 Goal Structure for $2(3x - 11) = 3x + 8$

and there is a parentheses operation specified on the left. We set up subgoal (4) to reduce the difference concerning the two x variables on the left side of the equation. The appropriate operation for this subgoal is *Combine variables*. Thus we set up subgoal (5) to apply this operator, but when we try we fail because we have not yet cleared up the parentheses. There is thus a difference (unfinished parentheses) that is noticed, so subgoal (6) is needed to reduce this difference. We find the operator *Compute parens* to be the relevant one, and set subgoal (7) to apply it. We succeed in applying this operator and create a new problem state. Thus subgoals (7) and (6) are popped off, and we return to subgoal (5). We can now apply the *Combine variables* operator and create another new problem state. Subgoals (5) and (4) pop off, and we return to the top goal. Again, we find a difference between the current state and the goal state, namely the fact that there is a number on the left. We create subgoal (8) to reduce this difference, and by consulting the condition–action chart we see that the appropriate operator is *Move number*. We set up a subgoal (9) to apply this operator. This succeeds, creates a new state, pops off subgoals (8) and (9), and returns us to the top goal. Now the solution path is fairly clear. Subgoal (10) is established to reduce the difference concerning two numbers on the right; subgoal (11) applies the *Combine numbers* operation to reduce that difference and create a new state ($3x = 30$). In trying the top goal again we find that there is a number on the left, so we seek to get rid of it [subgoal (12)] and apply the *Move number* operator [subgoal (13)] to produce a new state ($x = \frac{30}{3}$). Now we find that there are two numbers and a specified operation on the right, so we seek to eliminate that difference [subgoal (14)] and apply the *Combine numbers* operation [subgoal (15)]. When we return to the top goal we find that we have succeeded. This goal is popped off, and the problem is solved.

You might feel that this representation of the problem-solving process is a bit too tedious and detailed. However, the amount of detail is what makes this representational tool so useful and attractive. It is now possible to specify precisely and simply how someone goes about solving a problem. The means–ends analysis tool allows a much more precise description than simply saying that people tend to use goals in problem solving. It allows us to specify exactly how someone goes about using goals.

An important feature of the means–ends model described above is that it is testable. We can compare how the model performs with how a real person performs. If the model and the person produce quite different performances, then we must

---

1. Ugh. I hate algebra problems.
2. OK, let's see. Solve for x.
3. I can get rid of the $3x$ on this side (points to the right),
4. so I have to subtract $3x$ from both sides.
5. (Writes: $2(3x - 11) - 3x = 8$)
6. While I'm at it, I need to get the x's together,
7. but the parentheses are in my way.
8. I'll multiply first, $6x$ minus 22 (points to left side of equation).
9. (Writes: $6x - 22 - 3x = 8$)
10. Now I can get the x's together,
11. which makes $3x$,
12. and I have to get 22 out of there (points to left).
13. Three times x equals 22 plus 8.
14. Three times x equals 30,
15. so x equals 10.
16. That's it.

Box 5.9   Protocol for $2(3x - 11) = 3x + 8$

modify the model. If the person and the model produce quite similar performances, then we have some reason to think that we are on the right track.

In order to test our model, let's give our problem to a subject. Further, let's ask the subject to solve the problem aloud, telling us what he or she is thinking at each step in the problem. A protocol that consists of a written copy of the subject's statements is given in Box 5.9. Numbers are assigned to different statements for convenience.

How well does the subject's protocol fit the performance of the means–ends analysis model? In statements 1 and 2, the subject recognizes that this is an algebra solution problem. Thus, the subject is acting as if he is setting the goal of finding a value for x. In statement 3, the subject points out a difference that must be reduced and finds an operator [as in subgoal (2)]. In statement 4 the *Move variable* operator is applied [as in subgoal (3)] and in statement 5 a new state is created, as in the model. In statement 6, another difference is found [as in subgoal (4)], and in statement 7, there is a recognition of another problem [as in subgoal (5)]. In statement 8, a new operation is found [subgoal (6)] and in statement 9 it is successfully applied [subgoal (7)]. The rest of the protocol also follows the general order of the model. Statements 10 and 11 correspond to subgoals (12) and (13). Statements 14 and 15 correspond to subgoals (14) and (15). Statement 16 corresponds to the accomplishment of the original goal. Thus, it appears that the subject's protocol and the performance of the means–ends model are fairly similar.

The condition–action diagram in the above example was modified from the work of Bundy (1975). Bundy suggested that we should "read between the lines" in analyzing how people solve algebraic equations by examining the major subgoals they have. In the present example, we have created five different condition–action pairs that correspond roughly to those outlined by Bundy. Further, Bundy suggests that the GPS system of means–ends analysis could be applied to the process of equation solving, and provides some examples similar to those used above. Bundy also notes that GPS may have to be modified in order to describe the strategies used by humans; however, he offers no empirical test of his model.

In a recent series of experiments, Mayer, Larkin, and Kadane (1980) found evidence that college students did tend to use a means–ends analysis strategy in solving algebra equations like the example in this section. However, some of the problems were stated in words such as, "Find a number such that if 11 less than 3 times the number was doubled that would be the same as 8 more than 3 times the number." When problems were stated in words, subjects showed no signs of using a means–ends analysis strategy. Apparently, when information gets too complicated humans are not able to make use of planning techniques.

APPLYING WHAT YOU'VE LEARNED

Suppose that you ask a subject to solve the following algebra problem with paper and pencil:

$$5(2x) = 2 + 8x$$

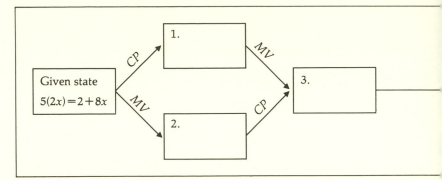

Box 5.10   Problem Space for $5(2x) = 2 + 8x$

The subject writes the following:

$$5(2x) = 2 + 8x$$
$$5(2x) - 8x = 2$$
$$10x - 8x = 2$$
$$2x = 2$$
$$x = 1$$

The subject also comments, "Always try to get the x's on the left and the numbers on the right first." Can you describe a means–ends analysis procedure that would have produced these states and that would be consistent with the subject's remark?

First, let's try to build a problem space so that we can see the paths that are available. Begin with the given state,

$$5(2x) = 2 + 8x$$

and see whether you can apply any of the five operators. Take a few minutes and try to build a problem space. If you have trouble, Box 5.10 provides a problem space for each of the states and gives the operation that leads to it. Can you fill in the states?

The correct states for Box 5.10 are as follows:

1. $10x = 2 + 8x$ 4. $2x = 2$
2. $5(2x) - 8x = 2$ 5. $x = \frac{2}{2}$
3. $10x - 8x = 2$ 6. $x = 1$

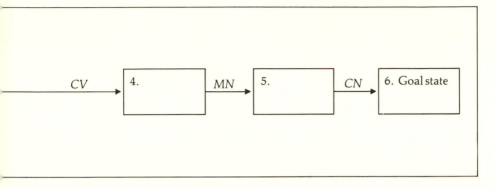

Now that you have built a problem space for the algebra equation problem, let's move on to the means–ends analysis. The same condition–action chart can be used as in Box 5.7. When selecting a difference to be reduced always try first to get the x's together on the left before making any computations with numbers. Box 5.11 provides a framework for this analysis. The top goal is to get a numerical value for x. Specify whether each subgoal is a *Transform*, a *Reduce*, or an *Apply*. If it is a *Transform*, tell what the major difference encountered is. If it is a *Reduce*, tell what the selected operator is. If it is an *Apply*, tell what the newly created state is. Can you fill in Box 5.11? Once you have filled it in, look at the analysis in Box 5.11a. Does your analysis look the same?

FURTHER APPLICATIONS OF STRATEGY MODELS

As you can see, there have been some exciting developments in the psychology of problem solving during the last decade. The beginning of this chapter described early research that suggested that humans use subgoals in problem solving (Duncker, 1945; Polya, 1957). This chapter has demonstrated two new tools for the analysis of problem solving—the problem space and the means–ends analysis of goal structure. These tools allow for a clear statement of the mechanism underlying the use of subgoals, and thus provide a real step forward over older, vaguer theories.

Subgoals in stack	Type of subgoal	Statement of subgoal	Success
(1)	*Transform*	Find value for x.	*No:* x on right, parens.

Box 5.11   Goal Structure for $5(2x) = 2 + 8x$

The pioneering work of Ernst and Newell (1969) and Newell and Simon (1972) demonstrated how a GPS-like system could be applied to a total of 14 different tasks. More recently, cognitive psychologists have been able to make improvements on the means–ends analysis system so that the model more closely fits the performance of human subjects. For example, Atwood and Polson (1976) successfully modified a GPS-like system for solving water jug problems so that they could more accurately predict the relative difficulty of problems. One change was to make some limitations on the system's memory. Egan (1973; Egan and Greeno, 1974) found that GPS was able to predict which steps in the tower of Hanoi problem would be most difficult; however, an even more accurate description could be derived by adding some memory limitations and allowing for more than one systematic planning strategy. Finally, work on a version of the missionaries and cannibals problem by several researchers (Thomas, 1974; Greeno, 1974; Simon and Reed, 1976) indicates that GPS-like systems fit the performance of subjects best when the task is fairly difficult, when the subject has some practice, and when hints are given. In other cases, subjects tend to use more variable strategies.

There have also been improvements in the techniques for generating a problem space. For example, Hayes and Simon's (1974) UNDERSTAND program takes a word problem and converts it into a problem space. The program has been applied to a wide variety of texts such as "instructions" and "directions." Earlier work by Bobrow (1968) produced a program that translated algebra story problems into a usable problem representation.

One useful direction for future research involves the analysis of problem-solving strategies in real-world domains. For example, Bundy (1975) analyzed the process by which people solve algebra equations. Greeno (1978) has analyzed the problem-solving strategies involved in geometry. Larkin (1979) has analyzed the strategies of experts and novices in solving physics problems. As techniques for representing strategies become more refined, we can expect fo find entire domains in mathematics and science mapped out.

As we learn more about the use of strategies in solving complex problems, we will be able to do a better job of teaching people how to solve problems. For example, Wickelgren's book *How to Solve Problems* (1974) provides instructions based on modern cognitive theory. As we are better able to describe the powerful, general heuristics that experts use, we may be able to devise ways of directly teaching these methods to novices.

Another future development may be that computer programs —designed by humans—may someday be able to beat humans in problem-solving exercises such as playing chess. A favorite topic of conversation among builders of problem-solving models concerns the date by which the best chess player in the world will be a computer program. Already, computer programs exist that can defeat very good chess players, but the grand masters are still humans as of this writing. In a recent issue of *Omni* researchers

Subgoals in stack	Type of subgoal	Statement of subgoal	Success
(1)	*Transform*	Find value for x.	No: x on right side, parens.
(2) (1)	*Reduce*	Get x on left.	Yes: Use *MV*.
(3) (2) (1)	*Apply*	Apply *MV*.	Yes: $5(2x) - 8x = 2$
(1)	*Transform*	Find value for x.	No: Two x's on left.
(4) (1)	*Reduce*	Get one x on left.	Yes: Use *CV*.
(5) (4) (1)	*Apply*	Apply *CV*.	No: Parens on left.
(6) (5) (4) (1)	*Reduce*	Eliminate parens.	Yes: Use *CP*.
(7) (6) (5) (4) (1)	*Apply*	Apply *CP*.	Yes: $10x - 8x = 2$
(5) (4) (1)	*Apply*	Apply *CV*.	Yes: $2x = 2$
(1)	*Transform*	Find value for x.	No: Number on left.
(8) (1)	*Reduce*	Get number on right.	Yes: Use *MV*.
(9) (8) (1)	*Apply*	Apply *MN*.	Yes: $x = \frac{2}{2}$
(1)	*Transform*	Find value for x.	No: Two numbers on right.
(10) (1)	*Reduce*	Get one number.	Yes: Use *CN*.
(11)(10) (1)	*Apply*	Apply *CN*.	Yes: $x = 1$
(1)	*Transform*	Find value for x.	Yes: $x = 1$. Stop.

Box 5.11a   Goal Structure for $5(2x) = 2 + 8x$. (One likely sequence of goals and subgoals.)

speculated that a machine will be the world champion within a few years. What this means is not that humans will have lost their place as thinkers in the world; quite the contrary, many cognitive psychologists will take pride in this event as evidence that the tools of science can successfully be applied to the study of the last frontier—the human mind.

SUGGESTED READINGS

Mayer, R. E., J. Larkin, and J. Kadane. *Analysis of the skill of solving algebra equations.* Santa Barbara, Calif.: University of California, Department of Psychology, Technical Report No. 80–2, 1980. Describes a system for representing the strategy a person uses in solving algebra equations.

Newell, A., and H. A. Simon. *Human problem solving.*
Englewood Cliffs, N.J.: Prentice-Hall, 1972. A highly
influential book that describes how means–ends analysis can
be used to represent human problem-solving performance.

Wickelgren, W. A. *How to solve problems: Elements of a
theory of problems and problem solving.* San Francisco:
W. H. Freeman and Company, 1974. Discusses the concepts
of problem space and means–ends analysis; provides
descriptions of the major problem-solving strategies.

References

Anderson, J. R., and G. H. Bower. *Human associative memory.* Washington, D.C.: Hemisphere Press, 1973.

Atwood, M. E., and P. G. Polson. A process model for water jug problems. *Cognitive Psychology,* 1976, *8,* 191–216.

Bartlett, F. C. *Remembering.* Cambridge: Cambridge University Press, 1932.

Bobrow, D. G. Natural language input for a computer problem-solving system. In M. Minsky (Ed.), *Semantic information processing.* Cambridge, Mass.: MIT Press, 1968.

Bransford, J. D. *Human cognition.* Belmont, Calif.: Wadsworth, 1979.

Brown. F. C. *Principles of educational and psychological testing.* New York: Holt, Rinehart & Winston, 1976.

Brown, J. S., and R. R. Burton. Diagnostic models for procedural bugs in basic mathematical skills. *Cognitive Science,* 1978, *2,* 155–192.

Brownell, W. A. Psychological considerations in learning and teaching arithmetic. In *The teaching of arithmetic: Tenth yearbook of the National Council of Teachers of Mathematics.* New York: Columbia University Press, 1935.

Bruner, J. S., J. J. Goodnow, and G. A. Austin. *A study of thinking.* New York: Wiley, 1956.

Bundy, A. *Analysing mathematical proofs.* Edinburgh: University of Edinburgh, Department of Artificial Intelligence, Research Report No. 2, 1975.

Buros, O. K. (Ed.). *Mental measurements yearbook.* (7 vols.) Highland Park, N.J.: Gryphon Press, 1938–1972.

Carpenter, P. A., and M. A. Just. Sentence comprehension: A psycholinguistic processing model of verification. *Psychological Review*, 1975, *82*, 45–73.

Chomsky, A. N. *Syntactic structures.* The Hague: Mouton, 1957.

Cofer, C. N. An historical perspective. In C. N. Cofer (Ed.), *The structure of memory.* San Francisco: W. H. Freeman and Company, 1976.

Detterman, D. K. A job half done: The road to intelligence testing in the year 2000. *Intelligence*, 1979, *3*, 295–306.

Duncker, K. On problem solving. *Psychological Monographs*, 1945, *58* (No. 270).

Ebbinghaus, H. *Memory.* New York: Dover, 1964. (Originally published in 1885.)

Egan, D. E. The structure of experience acquired while learning to solve a class of problems. Ann Arbor, Michigan: Department of Psychology, Doctoral Dissertation, 1973.

Egan, D. E., and J. G. Greeno. Theory of rule induction: Knowledge acquired in concept learning, serial pattern learning, and problem solving. In L. Gregg (Ed.), *Knowledge and cognition.* Hillsdale, N.J.: Erlbaum, 1974.

Ehrenpreis, W., and J. M. Scandura. Algorithmic approach to curriculum construction: A field test in mathematics. *Journal of Educational Psychology*, 1974, *66*, 491–498.

Ernst, G. W., and A. Newell. *GPS: A case study in generality and problem solving.* New York: Academic Press, 1969.

Fillmore, C. J. The case for case. In E. Bach and R. T. Harms (Eds.), *Universals in linguistic theory*. New York: Holt, Rinehart & Winston, 1968.

Greeno, J. G. Hobbits and orcs: Acquisition of a sequential concept. *Cognitive Psychology*, 1974, *6*, 270–292.

Greeno, J. G. A study of problem solving. In R. Glaser (Ed.), *Advances in Instructional Psychology*. New York: Wiley, 1978.

Groen, G. J., and J. M. Parkman. A chronometric analysis of simple addition. *Psychological Review*, 1972, *79*, 329–343.

Guilford, J. P. The three faces of intellect. *American Psychologist*, 1959, *14*, 469–479.

Guilford, J. P. *The nature of human intelligence*. New York: McGraw-Hill, 1967.

Hayes, J. R., and H. Simon. Understanding written instructions. In L. W. Gregg (Ed.), *Knowledge and cognition*. Hillsdale, N.J.: Erlbaum, 1974.

Hilgard, E. R., and G. H. Bower. *Theories of learning*. Englewood Cliffs, N.J.: Prentice-Hall, 1980.

Holtzman, T. G., R. Glaser, and J. W. Pellegrino. Process training derived from a computer simulation theory. *Memory and Cognition*, 1976, *4*, 349–356.

Horn, J. L. Trends in the measurement of intelligence. *Intelligence*, 1979, *3*, 229–240.

Humphrey, G. *Thinking: An introduction to its experimental psychology*. New York: Wiley, 1963.

Hunt, E. Varieties of cognitive power. In L. B. Resnick (Ed.), *The nature of intelligence*. Hillsdale, N.J.: Erlbaum, 1976.

Hunt, E. Mechanics of verbal ability. *Psychological Review*, 1978, *85*, 109–130.

Hunt, E., N. Frost, and C. Lunneborg. Individual differences in cognition: A new approach to intelligence. In G. Bower (Ed.), *The psychology of learning and motivation* (Vol. 7). New York: Academic Press, 1973.

Hunt, E., and M. Lansman. Cognitive theory applied to individual differences. In W. K. Estes (Ed.), *Handbook of cognitive processes: Introduction to concepts and issues* (Vol. 1). Hillsdale, N.J.: Erlbaum, 1975.

Hunt, E., C. Lunneborg, and J. Lewis. What does it mean to be high verbal? *Cognitive Psychology*, 1975, 7, 194–227.

Intelligence, 1979, 3, 215–306.

Kintsch, W. *The representation of meaning in memory.* Hillsdale, N.J.: Erlbaum, 1974.

Kintsch, W. Memory for prose. In C. N. Cofer (Ed.), *The structure of memory.* San Francisco: W. H. Freeman and Company, 1976.

Kintsch, W., and T. A. van Dijk. Toward a model of text comprehension and production. *Psychological Review,* 1978, 85, 363–394.

Landa, L. N. *Algorithmization of learning and instruction.* Englewood Cliffs, N.J.: Educational Technology Publications, 1974.

Larkin, J. H. Models of strategy for solving physics problems. Paper presented at annual meeting of the American Educational Research Association, 1979.

Lindsay, P. H., and D. A. Norman. *Human information processing: An introduction to psychology.* New York: Academic Press, 1977.

Mandler, J. M., and N. S. Johnson. Remembrance of things parsed: Story structure and recall. *Cognitive Psychology,* 1977, 9, 111–151.

Mandler, J. M., and G. Mandler. *Thinking: From association to gestalt.* New York: Wiley, 1964.

Mayer, R. E., and J. G. Greeno. Effects of meaningfulness and organization on problem solving and computability judgments. *Memory and Cognition*, 1975, *3*, 356–362.

Mayer, R. E., J. Larkin, and J. Kadane. *Analysis of the skill of solving equations.* Santa Barbara, Calif.: University of California, Department of Psychology, Technical Report No. 80–2, 1980.

Meyer, B. J. F. *The organization of prose and its effects on memory.* Amsterdam: North-Holland, 1975.

Miller, G. A. The magic number seven, plus or minus two. *Psychological Review*, 1956, *63*, 81–97.

Miller, G. A., E. Galanter, and K. H. Pribram. *Plans and the structure of behavior.* New York: Holt, Rinehart & Winston, 1960.

Minsky, M. A framework for representing knowledge. In P. H. Winston (Ed.), *The psychology of computer vision.* New York: McGraw-Hill, 1975.

Neisser, U. *Cognitive psychology.* New York: Appleton-Century-Crofts, 1967.

Newell, A., J. C. Shaw, and H. A. Simon. Elements of a theory of human problem solving. *Psychological Review*, 1958, *65*, 151–166.

Newell, A., and H. A. Simon. *Human problem-solving.* Englewood Cliffs, N.J.: Prentice-Hall, 1972.

Pellegrino, J. W., and R. Glaser. Cognitive correlates and components in the analysis of individual differences. *Intelligence*, 1979, *3*, 187–214.

Peterson, L. R., and M. J. Peterson. Short-term retention of individual verbal items. *Journal of Experimental Psychology*, 1959, *58*, 193–198.

Piaget, J. *The construction of reality in the child.* New York: Basic Books, 1954.

Polya, G. *How to solve it.* Garden City, N.Y.: Doubleday, 1957.

Polya, G. *Mathematical discovery.* New York: Wiley, 1968.

Posner, J., S. Boies, W. Eichelman, and R. Taylor. Retention of visual and name codes of single letters. *Journal of Experimental Psychology Monographs,* 1969, *79* (1, Pt. 2).

Potts, G. R. Information processing strategies used in the encoding of linear orderings. *Journal of Verbal Learning and Verbal Behavior,* 1972, *11,* 727–40.

Resnick, L. B. *The nature of intelligence.* Hillsdale, N.J.: Erlbaum, 1976a.

Resnick, L. B. Task analysis in instructional design: Some cases from mathematics. In D. Klahr (Ed.), *Cognition and instruction.* Hillsdale, N.J.: Erlbaum, 1976b.

Resnick, L. B. The future of I.Q. testing in education. *Intelligence,* 1979, *3,* 241–254.

Rumelhart, D. E. Notes on a schema for stories. In D. G. Bobrow and A. M. Collins (Eds.), *Representation and understanding: Studies in cognitive science.* New York: Academic Press, 1975.

Rumelhart, D. E. *Introduction to human information processing.* New York: Wiley, 1977.

Scandura, J. M. *Problem solving.* New York: Academic Press, 1977.

Schank, R. C., and R. P. Abelson. *Scripts, plans, goals, and understanding: An inquiry into human knowledge structures.* Hillsdale, N.J.: Erlbaum, 1977.

Simon, H. A., and K. Kotovsky. Human acquisition of concepts for sequential patterns. *Psychological Review,* 1963, *70,* 534–546.

Simon, H. A., and S. K. Reed. Modeling strategy shifts in a problem-solving task. *Cognitive Psychology,* 1976, *8,* 86–97.

Skinner, B. F. *Science and human behavior.* New York: Free Press, 1953.

Skinner, B. F. *About behaviorism.* New York: Knopf, 1974.

Spearman, C. General intelligence objectively determined and measured. *American Journal of Psychology,* 1904, *15,* 201–293.

Spearman, C. *The abilities of man.* New York: Macmillan, 1927.

Spilich, G. J., G. T. Vesonder, H. L. Chiesi, and J. F. Voss. Text processing of domain related information for individuals with high and low domain knowledge. *Journal of Verbal Learning and Verbal Behavior,* 1979, *18,* 275–290.

Stein, N. L., and T. Nezworski. The effects of organization and instructional set on story memory. *Discourse Processes,* 1978, *1,* 177–193.

Sternberg, R. J. *Intelligence, information processing, and analogical reasoning: The componential analysis of human abilities.* Hillsdale, N.J.: Erlbaum, 1977.

Sternberg, S. Memory-scanning: Mental processes revealed by reaction time experiments. *American Scientist,* 1969, *57,* 421–457.

Thomas, J. C., Jr. An analysis of behavior in the hobbits-orcs problem. *Cognitive Psychology,* 1974, *6,* 257–269.

Thorndike, E. L. *The psychology of learning.* New York: Columbia University Press, 1913.

Thorndike, E. L. *Human learning.* New York: Century, 1931.

Thorndyke, P. W. Cognitive structures in comprehension and memory of narrative discourse. *Cognitive Psychology,* 1977, *9,* 77–110.

Thurstone, L. L. *Primary mental abilities.* Chicago: University of Chicago Press, 1938.

Wallas, G. *The art of thought.* New York: Harcourt, 1926.

Wickelgren, W. A. *How to solve problems.* San Francisco: W. H. Freeman and Company, 1974.

Wolf, T. H. *Alfred Binet.* Chicago: University of Chicago Press, 1973.

Woods, S. S., L. B. Resnick, and G. J. Groen.
An experimental test of five process models for subtraction. *Journal of Educational Psychology,* 1975, *67,* 17–21.

Index